8-18-04

Lesley

Thanks for your help, you have a wonderful healing nature.

Brooks

Billy Blue and Other Plays

Brooks Tessier

VANTAGE PRESS
New York

To C. F. Adams and his great-granddaughter, Amy.

FIRST EDITION

All rights reserved, including the right of
reproduction in whole or in part in any form.

Copyright © 1995 by Brooks Tessier

Published by Vantage Press, Inc.
516 West 34th Street, New York, New York 10001

Manufactured in the United States of America
ISBN: 0-533-11153-6

Library of Congress Catalog Card No.: 94-90247

0 9 8 7 6 5 4 3 2 1

Contents

Billy Blue	1
Shattered Time	47
The Three Captains	83

Billy Blue

List of Characters

Eunice, socialite
Dax, son
Uncle Bud, Dax's uncle
Miles, cowboy
Lad, cowboy
Billy, Uncle Bud's illegitimate daughter
Crackers, Billy's mother
Cruiser, Billy's brother
Sharleen, Cruiser's girlfriend
Friend
Butlers
Soda Jerk
Judges
Rodeo Announcer
Sheriff

Act I

Scene i. *A sitting room*

An exclusive estate in the suburbs of Chicago. Dax, angular, handsome, in his twenties, sits with a friend sipping sloe gin fizzes. The life of the upper class is personified by the casualness of these two young men.

Friend (jokingly): Problem with you, Dax, is you've never had a real job. Neither have I, but I'm not worried about it. What's your problem? You have plenty of money. You've got life by the balls!
Dax: I want to do something meaningful with my life. I want to breathe fresh air and sweat real sweat. I want to feel blood pumping through my veins.
Friend: Listen to you; you'd last five minutes doing anything that required hard work.
Dax: You're crazy.

[*He sips his drink*]

I can handle hard work!
Friend: You'd be making excuses right and left about everything; it'd be your back, or your neck, or something.
Dax: There's more to life than hanging around country clubs and deb parties.
Friend: You've always talked that way and here you sit. Afraid to take the first step . . . Afraid to face the fact that this is the only life you can handle. Why don't you enjoy it? It's not so bad!
Dax: You think I'm afraid of hard work, getting my hands dirty, and being a worker?
Friend: That's right. You wouldn't last one week at a real job. You're just a discontented rich kid.

[*Butler enters*]

Butler: Dinner is being served.
Dax: We'll talk later.

Friend *leaves. Escorted by waiter, Dax enters a luxurious formal dining room with large oil paintings on the walls. Eunice, a well-preserved socialite, late fifties, sips her wine. Dax sits and studies his mother with sober sincerity; then his eyes fix on his crystal wine goblet, as he tries to avoid his mother's gaze.*

Eunice: Ever since your father died, you've gotten worse; and these ideas of yours, such ridiculous notions. Your father would never have put up with it!

[*She sips her wine*]

The Butler *enters and serves their plates from a silver tray.* Second Butler *enters.*

2nd Butler: A Ms. Feet is calling.
Eunice: Tell Ms. Feet I'm at the club.

[*Both butlers leave*]

I think you need to find something worthwhile to do with your life; then you'll appreciate what you have.

[*They eat*]

Dax: What do you want me to become, a politician, a lawyer, a doctor? Aren't there enough professional people in this country? I need a breath of fresh air.
Eunice: Stop your nonsense!

[*She sips her wine*]

Oh, I wish your father were here.
Dax: What about me going to work for Uncle Bud in Colorado?
Eunice: It's so uncivilized in the West, but of course your father would have liked the idea of your being with his brother.
Dax: It's a great idea!
Eunice: I suppose it wouldn't hurt. I'll write him when I get a chance.

[*She sips her wine*]

What if . . . I got you a job at the bank? Mr. Fink is quite fond of you.

[*Dax jumps up from the table*]

Dax: I'm going to call Uncle Bud.

[*Dax leaves the dining room*]

Scene ii. *The Paradise Valley Ranch*

Twenty thousand acres of deeded range land and a thirty-thousand-acre BLM lease of sage-brushed mountainside lie twenty miles east of Steamboat Springs, Colorado. Here the last of the Old West survives. Along the county road, thousands of cattle graze as the Yampa River meanders through the valley.

Driving his new pickup truck, Dax approaches the main ranch house. Uncle Bud, a muscular cowboy, fifties, scar on cheek, which makes upper lip curl, swings around from where he sits on the corral fence.

Bud: You're a sight!
 [*Dressed in city clothes, Dax gets out of the truck*]
 How about you; you look like your dad! Look how big you got!
 [*Bud pushes his hand forward and they shake*]
Dax: Nice to see you again, Uncle Bud.
 [*Bud puts his arm around Dax*]

Miles, *an aging cowboy, leads a stallion into the corral.* Lad, *a young cowboy, approaches* Bud.
Lad: Who's the city slicker?
Bud: This here's my nephew, Dax.
Lad: Howdy. Nice shiny truck.
 [*Lad laughs, showing his rotten and missing teeth*]
Miles (calling out): You breaking this new horse, Bud? Or maybe you're a little brittle to be getting into the saddle.
 [*The stallion jumps off the ground and bucks, Bud takes a long look at the stallion*]
Bud: I'll take him.

He takes off his jean jacket, puts it on the fence, and jumps into the corral.

Miles: Getting kinda old for this kinda work. You ain't no spring chicken.

Bud *takes the reins from* Miles *and talks softly to the horse. The stallion bucks as* Miles *moves off.*

Bud: Nice horsey.
> [*He runs his hand down the horse's shoulder*]

Now a nice boy like you can surely get along with a fellow like me. Ya see, we both got something in common, cowboying! I need you and you need me, 'cause without me, you wouldn't have a purpose, and we all need a purpose, don't we?

He takes a carrot out of his pocket and feeds the horse, then quickly swings into the saddle. The horse goes wild and begins to crow-hop, jarring every bone in Bud*'s body.* Dax *watches in disbelief.*

Lad: He's still pretty good, for fifty!
Miles: He's damn good!

The stallion bucks hard for some time then, begins to tire. Bud, *seeing his chance, jumps clear of the horse. He moves toward the corral fence, rubbing his lower back.*

Miles: Good one—you rode good!
Lad: He's a mean one. You ready for the next one, Bud?
> [*Lad laughs*]

Miles: Give him a break! C'mon, we got work to do!
> [*They wander toward the bunkhouse*]

Dax: I'm glad to be out of the city. I feel like everything's going to be okay now that I'm HERE! This place is great!
Bud: Apart from finding good help, taxes going up each year, and wolves eating the stock, it's all I could ask for.
> [*He stretches his back*]

I was never cut out for city life, all that confusion.

Naw, I can't live like that. It's bullshit, *PURE BULLSHIT*. I love this country. I wouldn't trade it for a million dollars!

[*He puts his hand on Dax's shoulder*]

So you want to be a cowboy, do ya? It ain't easy work and the hours are long, but it'll give you an education you'll never learn from books.

Miles is my head man; he'll be telling you the work that needs to be done. I told him to be easy on you at first.

Dax: I can handle it; I don't want any favors.

Bud: He'll treat you square! Your mother called last night. She wanted you to phone when you got here. Sounded like she missed you.

Dax: There's nothing for me back there.

Bud: Your dad thought I was crazy when I first came out to Colorado. I worked the truck yards in Denver a couple of winters. When there wasn't work there, I'd unload hundred-pound bags of salt from box cars. I saved some money and started a business, but I had a string of bad luck and lost everything. When I moved to the mountains, I started out punching cows. I got ahead and put some money down on this place.

Everything takes time, son, life isn't easy. One thing I'll tell ya, there's a *right* and a *wrong*. Nobody likes to admit it because folks would have to start *accounting* for their lives. I've tested it. If you mess around with somebody, somebody's going to mess around with you.

There's an old-line cabin on the mountain; she's all yours.

It will give you more privacy than being in the bunkhouse; we'll ride up tomorrow. First, we'll have to get you out of those clothes. They'll never do, especially those shoes. I'll look through some of my old things.

Dax: C'mon, Uncle Bud, I bet you wish you had a pair just like 'em.

[*Bud laughs*]

I'll get Mom to send you a pair.

Bud: How's Eunice?

Dax: Worse than ever. Biggest socialite you've ever seen.

Bud: She always was; she'll never change. When I was your age, I think I did everything imaginable. Wasn't nothing I didn't try. I didn't have a dime to my name. I remember one winter working for five dollars a day feeding cattle. Damn, it was cold. I thought about moving to Alaska for a while—gon'na try my hand at gold mining.

[*Bud pulls out a wolf-skin cap from his saddlebags*]

Dax: What is it?

Bud: The ole wolf skin.

[*Bud studies the cap, punches his fist into it, reshaping it, then puts it on*]

Now that was something else. I'll never forget that winter. I was out there feeding the cattle; the thermostat dropped to 40 degrees below zero. Man, it was a humdinger of a cold spell. Everyone was get'en cabin fever.

I was thirty years old then and driving a sleigh tote'n hay to the herd; it was about four o'clock, already started to get dark when this wolf comes out of nowhere.

Big wolf, he went one hundred seventy-five pounds; this thing hits me in the back, felt like a Mack truck hit me.

[*He squishes the cap*]

Boom, I'm in the snow, head down.

[*Bud takes the cap off his head and studies it*]

That's him . . . that's the wolf, skinned 'em, (*looking crazy*) . . . That's the wolf. Lucky Boy! That's what *they* called me. It's yours for luck.

[*He tosses the cap to Dax. They start for the ranch house*]

Dax: How come you never married?

Bud: I wanted to marry, but I was one of those drifting hard-headed cowboys, who never wanted to settle down. Then I met this gal. We had a baby girl, cutest thing you've laid eyes on.

Everything was going along just fine when she got the roving eye for another cowboy; damn shame how it all turned out, damn shame! C'mon, let's get us a drink. I'm as dry as a bone.

[*They go inside*]

Scene iii. *The range*

Bud *and* Dax *ride the range. The air is cold and the horses' breath freezes as it comes out their nostrils. Entering a thicket of aspens, the orange and red leaves create an imaginary landscape; yellow shapes float aimlessly around them. The silence is broken by motorcycles racing through a pristine meadow; the horses spook.*

Bud: Whoa! Whoa!

[*Bud calms the horses*]
    Sometimes I think horses have more sense than people. We've been having a lot of trouble these last couple of years, folks thinking they can trespass on someone's land, cut fences. There's just no respect for private property! Some of these newcomers are plumb crazy. No common sense!

[*He takes a wad of chew and puts it in his mouth*]
    There's a resort not far from here; developers want to buy this land for building condominiums. There's something about this country that most people don't understand. They usually have to learn the hard way.

Dax *takes a deep breath and drinks in the timelessness of the range.*

Bud: Nothing changes, it's like the truth.
Dax: This is great.

Jagged mountain peaks loom in the background as they approach a weathered line cabin.

Bud: I use to live up here when I was your age. Best years of my life. It made me slow down and really see things.
Dax (jokingly): What does a guy do for fun around here?
Bud: You'll be busy, there's plenty of firewood to chop, fence to fix, and stray cows to corral.
Dax (slightly nervous): Anything else I should know?

Bud: You know how to start a fire?

[*Dax nods*]

Good. I had the boys stock the cabin with food; I'll have them come up next week to check on ya. Well, this is it! Ain't it a beauty!

They dismount and corral their horses. Bud *removes a shotgun from his scabbard.*

Bud (smiling): You know how to use a shotgun?
Dax (anxious): Never have!
Bud: Well, it's about time you learned! It's my lucky gun; it got the *BIG WOLF*.
Dax: I won't need it, will I?
Bud: Never can tell in this country. Here's a box of shells. Try loading it.

Bud *tosses* Dax *a box of shells and the gun, then pulls a bottle of whiskey out of his saddlebags and opens it. He takes a gulp.*

Bud: You'll like it here.
[*Bud takes another gulp as Dax loads the shotgun*]
It's good for your blood.
[*He takes a drink and shivers*]
Bud: Just keep your eyes open for wolves; they start coming down this time of the year.

Scene iv. *Line cabin*

Bud *and* Dax *enter the cabin, which is sparsely furnished, a fireplace at one end and a kitchen at the other.* Bud *takes a kerosene lamp off the kitchen shelf and lights it. The room slowly comes to life.*

Bud: You'll figure the cabin out in no time; the place is pretty self-explanatory.

Dax *looks about nervously, realizing his new reality, living alone on the side of a mountain.*

Dax: I never imagined it would be like this. I mean, this is very rustic.
Bud (smiling): You expect some kinda Hilton Hotel?
[*Bud opens the cabinets*]
Bud: Knives and forks, plates, pots and pans, you got everything you need.
[*Dax slumps onto the couch*]
Something bothering you? You seem to have grown a little pale in the cheeks.
Dax: I'm just a little worn out from the ride.
Bud: Good. I was afraid for a minute there you were getting homesick. Well, I best be getting back before dark.

Bud *starts out of the cabin and* Dax *follows, clutching the shotgun.*

Bud: Good luck.
[*They shake hands and Bud mounts his horse*]
Be careful with that shotgun; don't be shooting yourself in the foot.

As Bud *rides off, ravens fly wild, frightened by the sound of something moving through the brush.* Dax *cautiously takes aim with the loaded shotgun and nervously stands guard. A stallion emerges from a thicket of cottonwoods and moves forward.*

From behind the cabin, Billy, a young woman in her twenties, surprises him; he wheels around and aims the shotgun at her.

Dax: Sorry, I thought I heard wolves.
[*He lowers the gun*]
You surprised me.
Billy: Something wrong with me being here?
Dax: No. Don't get me wrong.
[*Dax searches for words*]

Bud Moon's my uncle. I'm here to help out on the ranch. I'll be living here in the cabin.
Billy: Oh, I see.

A cold wind blows and her hair flies wild. Dead leaves float by.

Billy: Nice to meet you.
    [*She walks toward her horse and swings onto his back*]
Dax: What's your name?
Billy: Billy. See you around.
                                            [*She rides off*]

Act II

Scene i. *A toy store*

Stuffed animals and lifelike puppets dangle from the ceiling as if in effortless dance. The diffused light entering the only window reveals the somber mood of a store where children could seldom be found. In the dimly lit corner, we find Crackers, *an elderly, absentminded woman absorbed in sweeping the wooden floor.*

A rat runs across the floor and she tries to beat it with her broom, but it escapes under the cabinet.

Crackers: Damn!

She gets on her hands and knees and pokes the end of the broom into the rat's lodge. The bell above the door rings, and Billy *enters.*

Billy (calling): Mom?
Crackers: Back here!
[*She continues to poke at the Rat's lodge as Billy approaches*]
Billy: Everything okay?
Crackers: Same damn rat.
         [*She stands up*]
  You have a nice ride, honey?
Billy: I went up on the mountain, where you used to take me
  when I was a little girl. It's so beautiful with all the colors.
       [*Crackers dusts off the stuffed animals*]
  It's cold in here!
Crackers: Oh?

Crackers *hobbles between the aisles, followed by* Billy. *They approach a large pot-bellied stove and warm themselves.* Crackers *holds both hands close to the stove.*

Crackers: When you get to be my age, every inch of your body aches when it starts cooling down.

Crackers *turns up the radio and gutturally mimics the words of the song.*

Crackers: That's Billy Holiday.
[*She absentmindedly looks off*]
The radio says it's supposed to get REAL cold. It's just not normal living when the temperature gets below zero.
[*Crackers turns up the volume on the radio*]
Billy: This music is depressing.
Crackers: You young people listen to such crap these days.
Billy: I'm going upstairs. Come up when you're ready to eat. I'll make you some dinner.
Crackers: Cruiser stopped by looking for you. I know how you feel about him, but he's your brother; everybody likes him! He's just a little mixed up; you have to be patient with him.
Billy: Why can't he leave me alone? He frightens me.
Crackers: Men are like that.
[*She sways and loses her balance. Billy steadies her*]
Help me to the couch.

Billy *supports her, they move to the back of the store and* Crackers *sits down.*

Crackers: You were always so shy as a child, living in your own world. You have to learn not to be so sensitive, honey. Everything will be all right.
[*Crackers takes a bottle of Valium from her apron*]
Here, take a Valium.
Billy: No, thanks.
[*Crackers swallows a couple of Valium*]
Crackers: They always help me. You need to remember he's been through hell this past year and a half in the pen. He didn't deserve what he got. He's got stuff to work out, sure, but don't we all.

Billy: I've tried to understand him, but he doesn't treat me as a sister. He acts like I'm a whore.
Crackers: Stop that talk, you hear me? I won't listen to it.
[*Billy starts for the back stairs*]
Billy: Talk to him before it's too late.
[*She goes upstairs*]

Scene ii. *A small, stark room overlooking a flashing stoplight and Main Street; kitchenette at end of room; fifties-style aluminum formica table and chairs*

Billy *turns up the thermostat on upright wall furnace, then moves across the room and closes the drapes. The changing colors of the stoplight can be seen through the transparent window coverings.*

She switches on a sixteen-inch black and white TV and opens the closet. "Truth or Consequences" materializes on the set, but is drowned out by the sound of the furnace switching on and off.

She undresses. In bra and panties, Billy *stands in front of the kitchen sink and washes her hands and face. Wetting a sponge, she sits back on the table and sponge-bathes her body. She takes a straight-edge razor from above the sink and shaves her legs.*

The door opens and Crackers *enters with* Billy's *cat.*

Crackers: It's just me, honey.
Billy: Make yourself comfortable.

Billy *goes to the closet and puts on a worn, stained bathrobe.*

Crackers: Do you have any whiskey?
Billy: Look in the cabinet over the fridge. Sugar Paws, where have you been? I was worried about you.

She pets the cat. Crackers *takes down a bottle of Black Velvet and a shot glass; she opens the whiskey and pours the shot glass full to the top. She drinks it down greedily.*

Crackers: Want one?
Billy: Not right now.

Crackers *pours another and sits at the kitchen table. She takes a package of cigarettes from her apron and pulls one out. She lights the cigarette and draws the smoke deeply into her lungs. She coughs, then downs another shot of whiskey.*
    Billy *continues to pet* Sugar Paws.

Crackers: Damn cat, always a problem.
Billy (to cat): Sugar Paws, you're a nice kitty.

Crackers *pours another shot, with her cigarette dangling from her lips. She moves toward the television and turns off the volume.*

Crackers: What are you going to do now that you're home? I wish you called and talked to me about dropping out of college.
Billy: Something wasn't right inside me. I felt all mixed up.
Crackers: I can't believe you. You kids only think about yourselves. When do you think I last heard from my brother? He hasn't called in over a month. I don't know where the hell he is!
Billy: He's always been that way; it never seemed to bother you before.
Crackers: I'm almost fifty-six years old. You kids don't have any respect.
Billy: Please, Mother, not now.
                  [*Crackers moves toward the kitchen table*]
Crackers: You don't care.
   [*The cat rubs up against Crackers's leg. She kicks it away*]
        Damn cat, snagged my new nylons.
Billy: I'm sorry about the way things worked out with college.
Crackers: I ain't hungry. I'll see you in the morning.

No sooner does she leave than Cruiser *pushes in the backdoor.*

Cruiser: I heard you came back. I'm sorry about what happened before you left for college.
Billy: I don't want to talk about it again. Please leave me alone. I'm tired of the way you treat me!
Cruiser: You shouldn't talk like that!
Billy: Well, it's true.
[*Cruiser tries to grab her*]
Leave me alone!
Cruiser: Leave me alone, leave me alone! What kind of shit is that? I'm your brother! Don't you think I care about you? Your business is my business!
Billy: I don't want you around. Go away!
Cruiser: And who's going to make me?
Billy: Get out!
Cruiser: I don't believe you really mean that, you sweet thing.
[*He grabs her and pulls her close*]
Billy: Get your hands off me!

He rips her bathrobe open and knocks her to the floor. He jumps on top of her.

Billy: You filthy pig!

Using his full weight, he forces her flat against the floor. She struggles, but is unable to restrain him. Her fight slowly leaves as he fondles her. Eyes closed and lifeless, she remains sprawled on the floor. He stands.

Cruiser: You know you loved every minute of it, you slut.

Billy *remains motionless for some time after* Cruiser *leaves; she staggers to her feet and smoothes her hair with the palm of her hand.* Crackers *enters.*

Crackers: I thought I heard some noise up here.

[*Billy stares at her*]
What's wrong, girl? Ain't you got no ears?
[*Billy cries*]
My God! What's wrong now! I'll be damned if you don't always got the problems. Now stop all the theatrics and come to your senses, gal. What is it? I'm no mind reader, ya know!
Billy: Cruiser was here, he hit me.
Crackers: You got to be kidding. Don't that boy have no sense? I never would have thought it of him. You sure you didn't lead him on? You're a strong girl. How could you let him do it?
[*Billy cries*]
I don't believe it; he doesn't act suppressed or whatever the word for it is. Did he hurt you?
Billy: No.
Crackers: Why then, it was probably half your fault, girl.
Billy: I tried to fight him off!
Crackers: Oh, hell! I'd just forget the whole thing as if it didn't happen. It'd be different if he did it out in the middle of the street in front of everybody. Just forget it, honey. That's the way I'd deal with the situation. You don't want to create a big stink and cause trouble.
[*Billy looks at her mother in disbelief*]
Billy: You want me to pretend *nothing happened!* What's wrong with you? *Don't you understand?*

Crackers *turns on the TV and gets a game show. She turns up the volume.*

Crackers: This here show will lift your spirits. Wouldn't it be fun to get on a show like that?
[*She sits and watches TV. Billy gets up and puts on her overcoat*]
Billy: I'm going to tell the sheriff!
Crackers: The hell you are, girl. I'll deny everything!
Billy: You've always turned your back; he's never had any discipline. I remember when he was a teenager and stole

a car. You swore to the police he never left home that night. You can't always cover up for him.
Crackers: He was just a boy then. He didn't know any better.
Billy: My God! Look what you've turned him into.

Crackers *gets up, moves toward* Billy, *and slaps her across the face.*

Crackers: Don't you *ever* talk about my boy like that.

Lifelessly, Billy *removes her overcoat and lets it fall to the floor.*

    Scene iii. *Drug store*

Dax *and* Bud *sit at the soda fountain, sipping coffee.*

Soda Jerk: It's shaping up to be a cold, hard winter.
Bud: It sure is.
Soda Jerk: I'm going to Miami in January, gonna take me a *real* vacation.
    [*He sponges off the counter and moves off*]
Bud: What do you plan on doing?
Dax: I'd like to stay on for the winter. I met this girl at the cabin, a local girl named Billy. She's beautiful!
Bud: Sure, I know her. She's always attracted attention. She's the one I told you about, the cute little girl I had out of wedlock. I would have liked to raise Billy; problem was, I couldn't handle her mother. She's a high-spirited little gal! She's been brought up hard.
    [*He watches Dax out of the corner of his eye*]
    She's a humdinger, she is. It'll be a lucky man that ends up with her. Now just keep everything I've told you under your hat!
    [*Billy enters*]
    Well, I'll be hog-tied. We was just talking about you.
    [*He stands and gives her a bear hug*]
    Look at you, more beautiful than ever, best-looking

filly this side of the Rockies. If I were twenty years younger, I'd marry you.

Dax: Nice to see you again, Billy.

Billy: Same here. I need to talk to you, Bud, if you don't mind.

Dax: I got errands to do. See you later, Billy.

[*He leaves*]

Billy: Cruiser came by last night, forced his way into my apartment.

[*She starts to cry*]

Bud: Talk to me, Billy.

Billy: You swear if I tell you, you won't breathe a word of it?

Bud: I swear.

Billy: Cruiser hit me. I don't know what to do about him.

Bud: Have you told the sheriff?

Billy: Ma won't hear of it. She said she'd deny everything.

Bud: I'd give anything to get my hands on that son-of-a—

Billy: You swore to leave it be.

Bud: I don't know what to say. Is there anything I can do?

Billy: I've had all my feelings locked up inside; it feels good just to tell someone. At first, I felt so angry and resentful. Now, I feel sorry for him, he's so mixed up!

I need to find someplace to live. I've got to move.

Bud: You can stay up in the line cabin with my nephew.

Billy: What about him?

[*He winks*]

Bud: I'll put in the good word for you. He'll listen to me. He likes you.

Billy: I knew you'd help me.

She leaves. Bud *paces back and forth then uses the phone to call* Crackers. *He orders another coffee and waits.* Crackers *enters and sits down across from* Bud. *No one speaks. The* Soda Jerk *breaks the silence.*

Soda Jerk: Howdy-do?

Crackers: Don't howdy-do me! Just go do something so we can talk *private*.

[*Soda Jerk moves off*]

What's so *damn* important you needed to talk to me?
Bud: It's about Cruiser.
Crackers: Let's not get into that again.
Bud: Cruiser's headed for trouble. He's like a stick of dynamite getting ready to explode. He'll end up back in the slammer. There'll be trouble before it's over; you can bet on that!
Crackers: He seems fine to me. It's Billy, *your daughter*, that I got hell with.

Ever since she came back from college, she thinks she knows it all.

She expects *me* to *feed* and clothe her on what I make! She's the no-good one if you ask me! Billy's got that no-good blood of yours. That *damn* cowboy that got me pregnant with Cruiser. I'd like to have shot him wherever in hell he is! Anything else you be wanting to educate me about?
Bud: You never could listen to reason.
Crackers: I never met a man that was straight with me.
Bud: C'mon, every time we used to talk and there was something you didn't agree with, you'd go stomping off to some bar and get drunk.
Crackers: I don't have to listen to this.
Bud: I remember when you left me high and dry for Freddy Palmer; you thought he was the *King of Cowboys, Prince Freddy.* Personally I think he fell off of too many bulls, landed on his brains until they didn't work anymore!

[*She hobbles off*]

Scene iv. *Line cabin*

Firewood is scattered about as Dax *splits log rounds. He is continually getting the ax stuck and expends all of his energy trying to remove the tool from the wood. Fatigued, he sits on the ground to rest.* Billy *approaches on horseback.*

Dax: Nice to see you again.
[*Billy dismounts and corrals her horse*]

Billy: I guess Bud told you I was coming.

Dax: He said you needed a place to stay for a while. I'm happy to have some company; it gets pretty quiet around here without someone to talk to.

Billy: I brought some food; figured you could use a good home-cooked meal; men aren't much good at cookin' for themselves.

Dax: You got that right.

She releases the saddlebags and pulls them down off the horse.

Dax: I never had to cook at home.

Billy: I'm surprised you've stayed this long here. I didn't figure a city kid to last.

Dax: I didn't really have much of a choice; it was either this or Chicago and there was no way I was going back there.

Billy: What kinda work did you do there?

                    [*Dax picks up a stick and draws in the dirt*]

Dax: A little bit of everything.

Billy: So, you were just hanging out?

Dax: I guess you would call it that. I never figured out what I was supposed to do; it wasn't that I was lazy, but I just didn't find my thing.

Billy: I know what you mean. I tried going to college and getting a degree in psychology, but it just made my mind more confused till I thought I was going crazy. In my book, anybody who wants to go around analyzing everything is weird. I'm just working on making my mind quiet. Sometimes I get things so jumbled up in my head I want to scream.

Dax: Yeah, that's the way it is for me, I guess. That's why I'm here. The solitude helps me put things into perspective.

Billy: Sounds like we'll get along just fine. Now, where are your manners? Aren't you going to help me with my gear?

He takes the saddlebags from her, and they start for the cabin.

Scene v.

The sun is directly overhead as Dax *sits on a boulder and studies the slow moving creek. He hears the sounds of* Billy *singing. Curiously, following the sound, he walks beside the creek and comes upon her.*

Billy (surprised): What are you doing? *(pause)* What do you want?
    [*She tosses a smooth rock skimming across the water*]
Dax: Mind if I sit down?
    [*Billy skips another stone*]
    I heard you singing, it surprised me.
Billy: If you don't mind, I need to figure some things out. Sort some things out in my head. I need some space.
    [*Dax starts to leave*]
    Wait.
    [*Dax turns*]
    Please, come back.
Dax: Don't you like me?
Billy: You're okay.
Dax: You want to talk?
    [*He sits next to her*]
Billy: Since I was fourteen men have come on to me.
    [*She skips a stone*]
    I'm tired of being used. All you men want is one thing!
Dax: C'mon.
Billy: Well, it's true!
Dax: You shouldn't talk like that. I don't feel that way about you. I don't understand.
Billy: I know you don't. Since I've been home all my ma does is nag, nags all the time. Maybe I don't know where I'm going with my life, but I'll figure it out.
Dax: I know how you feel.
    [*Billy searches his eyes*]
Billy: Do you like yourself?
Dax: Sure, I guess *(pause)*. What about you?
Billy: No.

[*She begins to cry. He moves closer*]

Dax: You okay?
Billy: I'm just sad.
Dax: Listen, I got an idea. Suppose to be a big to-do at the fairgrounds. How 'bout you and me going to town.
Billy: I don't know.
Dax: It'll be fun, c'mon, Bud will be there!
Billy: I suppose.

Scene vi.

The town of Steamboat Springs is celebrating at the fairgrounds. The bleachers are crowded with Spectators *watching the bull riding event.* Lad *struggles to get on the bull while* Cowboys *restrain the animal in the pen.*

Rodeo Announcer (over P.A.): Lad Ricker will be riding for the Paradise Valley Ranch. Good luck, Lad.

Clown *opens the gate to the pen and the bull comes out bucking.* Lad *gets thrown in less than five seconds.*

Rodeo Announcer: Let's give Lad a hand folks, that's one mean bull. Better luck next time, cowboy.

Lad *limps toward the gate.*
Behind the main arena a Girl *in a bikini sits on a platform above a pool, next to her is a target. A* Cowboy *hurls a baseball and misses. He throws another and hits the target squarely. The* Girl *drops into the pool and the excited* Cowboy *takes off his boots and jumps into the pool after her.*
Down the way Judges *move among* Contestants, *tasting chili.* Dax *stands behind a table next to* Bud, *who is wearing a big white cook's hat and slicing some peppers.*

Dax: You're a man of many talents.

Bud: I cook some of the best chili you ever ate. I've won two cook-offs.
   [*He searches his pocket and produces newspaper clippings*]
      Here it is, black and white.
Dax: Let me see that!
                    [*Bud stirs the chili while Dax reads*]
Bud: This is a hot batch. My chili was so hot last year it made the Judge sweat tears under his eyeballs. This is even hotter!

The Judges *approach.*

First Judge: You ready, Bud?
Bud: Ready, Judge!

The two Judges *put out their plates and* Bud *scoops a large ladle full of chili from his cooker and puts some on the* First Judge's *plate. He does the same for the other. The* Judges *taste the chili.*

First Judge: Clearly, this is the best chili I've tasted.
Second Judge: It's the hottest!

Second Judge *begins to sweat under his eyeballs.* Bud *pours him a glass of ice water. The* First Judge *signals for water.* Bud *pours.*

First Judge: I think you've done it again, Bud. Three years in a row, isn't it?
Bud: That's right.

The Second Judge *hands the first place ribbon to* Bud.

Bud: Thank you, thank you very much.
      [*He shakes hands with the Judges. The Judges leave*]
Dax: Good going.
Bud: You see that judge sweating?

Billy *approaches.*

Billy: What did they tell you?
Bud: Best chili they ever tasted.
> [*He shows her the first-place ribbon*]

Bud: Let's go find us some cold beer, we got some celebrating to do!

Bud *takes off his chef's hat and they start for an open-air bar. The temporary bar is about fifty feet long, made of plywood and set on sawhorses. Cowboys and Girls sit at the tables and chairs scattered about the field. Beyond is an old, makeshift, wooden dance floor and bandstand. Bud, Dax and Billy take a table and a* Waitress *follows with a pitcher of beer. A bluegrass band comes on stage and begins to play. Cowboys* HOOT.

At a far table, Billy's *brother,* Cruiser, *sits alone.*

Bud: How come you're so quiet, Billy?
Billy: I'm just thinking.
> [*Bud sips his beer*]

Bud: You need to let down some of your walls. What's bothering you?
Billy: What are you talking about? (*pause*) I'm getting out of here!
[*Bud puts his hand on her shoulder as she tries to stand*]
Bud: C'mon, Billy, just relax. I won't talk about it again. (*to Dax*) You ever think about getting married, raising a family?
Dax: I don't think I'd be very good at it. Marriage doesn't make any sense to me. Being single suits me just fine.
> [*Bud winks at Billy*]

Billy: Excuse me. I've got to use the facilities.

She starts through the crowd. Cruiser *spots her and starts toward her, blocking her way.*

Cruiser: Something wrong, Billy?
Billy: Leave me alone. Can't you get that into your thick skull?
Cruiser: I don't believe you really mean that, you sweet thing.
Billy: Just get your ass out of my way.

[*He grabs her*]

   Get your hands off me!

Bud *sees* Billy *in a heated argument with* Cruiser. *He approaches.*

Bud: What's wrong, Billy?
Billy: He won't leave me alone.
Cruiser: I don't think this is any of your business, Bud.
Bud: I'm making it my business, Cruiser. Now leave the lady be!
Cruiser: And who's going to make me?

[*Bud rolls up his shirt sleeve and makes a fist*]

Bud: This little fist, right here.

He swings and hits Cruiser, *knocking him onto the ground. Cowboys gather around.* Cruiser *feels his jaw as he slowly gets to his feet.*

Bud: C'mon Billy, it's time to go.

[*Cruiser grabs her.*]

Cruiser: I didn't say you could go.

[*Billy breaks free of his hold and moves through the crowd*]

Cruiser: Hit me again if you got the guts!
Bud: No shit!

[*Bud knocks Cruiser senseless*]

Cowboy: He's had enough!

Act III

Scene i. *Open range*

Dax *is caught in a snowstorm; he forces his horse into a thicket of trees and dismounts. He observes a herd of deer coming down the ridge and across a meadow. They move into an aspen grove and the leader sniffs the air; the herd moves through the trees and out of sight.*

Not *seeing any break in the storm,* Dax *forces his horse forward and leads the animal into the blizzard.*

Inside the line cabin, Billy *places kindling on top of newspaper, then strikes a match, lighting the fire. The flame quickly spreads among the dry wood scraps; the fire begins to crack.*

Dax *forces the door open. He moves next to* Billy *and warms himself by the fire.*

Dax: The storm caught me by surprise. Man, it's cold out there. You have anything warm to drink?

Billy *gives him a blanket off the couch, then goes to heat coffee.* Dax *grabs the whiskey off the shelf.*

Dax: Antifreeze.
                                           [*He takes a gulp!*]
My feet feel like a couple of ice cubes. I can't even feel my toes.

He puts the bottle down and raises his hands directly over the flames.

Billy: Careful!
Dax: My hands are frozen; they feel like someone is sticking pins into them.
Billy: Shake them out; they'll come around, probably sting for a while.

She takes the boiling coffee off the woodstove and pours him a cup.

Dax: I've never been in a blizzard.
Billy: Listen to you.
　　　　　　　　　　　　[*She puts her hand to his face*]
　　　　It's just a little snowstorm.
　　　　　　　　　　　　　　　　　[*She laughs*]
　　　　You're too much.
　　　　　　　　　　　　　　　[*He starts to warm*]
Dax: When I was in the city, I felt like everybody was crazy. Like I was normal and everybody else was ABNORMAL, except maybe it's me that's abnormal and they're NORMAL.
Billy: I know how you feel. When I'm in a city, it makes me feel like a cat in a cage.
　　　　　　　　　　　　　[*She moves close to Dax*]
　　　　You have kind eyes; they say the eyes are the mirror of your soul.
　　　　　　[*She searches his eyes, then changes the subject*]
　　　　How long do you think this storm will keep up?
Dax: Looks like there's at least ten inches of new snow; the thermometer says 20 degrees. Going to get cold tonight.
Billy: I don't like being out at night, too dangerous. A person could freeze to death.

She moves back from Dax and sits on the couch. He moves next to her and tries to kiss her.

Billy: You stay where you are. I told your Uncle Bud I'd try and understand you. I didn't promise anything else.
　　　　　　　　　　　　　　　[*He touches her gently*]
Dax: Are you afraid?
Billy: Afraid . . . No . . . I feel safe. I'm just sad.
Dax: What's wrong?
Billy: Nothing.
Dax: I swear, Billy, I wish I knew what went on inside that head of yours.

Billy: I need to talk to you about something that happened to me, but promise you won't tell Bud!

Dax: Promise.

Billy: When I was seventeen, Cruiser forced me into his car and raped me. At first, I felt nothing; there wasn't a lot of emotion. Then the feelings came. I started to jerk and flinch in my sleep. As time passed, my neck and shoulders knotted, my stomach cramped. I'd cry uncontrollably at unexpected times. One night after a movie that showed blood, I became sick.

Cruiser frightens me. The way he's been acting, he has that look in his eyes again.

Dax: I'll protect you. I won't let him hurt you.

Scene ii. *Cruiser's apartment*

The flames from the fireplace grow as Cruiser *plays his banjo.* Crackers *extends her hands forward to warm them. The glow from the fire reveals her sad face.*

Crackers: Oh, son, you could have been a star!

[*Crackers stirs the fire*]

Crackers: Who's the girl in the song?

Cruiser: Just some girl.

Crackers: How are you and Mary getting on?

Cruiser: She's not my type. I need to find somebody more sophisticated.

[*Cruiser strums*]

Crackers: Billy told me you hit her, told me you was no good!

Cruiser: I wouldn't touch her now with a ten-foot pole! She's no good!

Crackers: You got that right. Don't worry, son, you'll meet someone. You're special!

Remember when you were a kid? . . . You always learned quicker than the other boys; ya made me proud. I won't forget the time you rubbed that Smith boy's nose in the mud.

[*She laughs, then has a coughing fit*]
Remember when you won the silver buckle for junior rodeo?

Cruiser: Those were the days! I couldn't do nothing wrong then.

[*Cruiser strums the banjo*]

Crackers: Damn sister of yours, ain't got no respect. She's moved out to Bud's old cabin on the mountain. She said she wanted some space, whatever in hell that means. You bring her back, son.

[*He smiles to himself*]

Cruiser: Sure.
Crackers: The sheriff stopped by looking for you.
Cruiser: Oh? What the hell's wrong now?

Someone knocks at the door and Sharleen *pops her head in the front door.*

Sharleen: Hello.
Crackers: Oh, no it's her! Night, sweetie, time for me to go.

Crackers *ignores* Sharleen *and goes out the door.* Sharleen *enters wearing tight jeans and a cowgirl shirt, half-buttoned to show off her cleavage.*

Sharleen: I was just talking to some cowgirls from Wyoming. Is it true what they say?
Cruiser: What did they tell you?
Sharleen: They said you danced four gals into the ground, then you took 'em home and finished them off!
Cruiser (smiling): Nothing but hearsay.
Sharleen: Aren't you the stud, packin' the BIG Gun?
Cruiser: Well, maybe you'll see.
Sharleen: Is it true about those Wyoming gals?
Cruiser: Let's have us some whiskey. We got some celebrating to do!

Cruiser *grabs the bottle of whiskey and a couple of glasses off the counter.*

Sharleen: How long were you in for?
Cruiser: Year and a half.
Sharleen: Did you do it?
Cruiser: Damn right I did it and I'd do it again!
[*Sharleen hoots*]
Sharleen: Bartender, I'll buy this man a whiskey.
[*Cruiser pours her a stiff one and one for himself*]
Sharleen: Here's to you.
[*They down the whiskey*]
Cruiser: You sweet thing.

Her thick lips part, showing her uneven teeth. She touches his shoulder and runs her hand down his arm.

Sharleen: You gonna buy me another?
[*Cruiser serves Sharleen*]
Cruiser: You *are* beautiful.
[*Sharleen drinks her whiskey*]
Cruiser: I'd do anything for you.
Sharleen: C'mon now! You trying to sweet-talk me.

Sharleen *drunkenly knocks her glass over.* Cruiser *pours her another whiskey.*

Sharleen: My ma thinks I should become a PROFESSIONAL model. Dad's afraid they'll try to get me to pose without any clothes.
Cruiser: Would you do it?
Sharleen: Pose nude? I don't think so. I mean, I wouldn't pose without my panties. I'd never show that!
[*She drinks*]
Cruiser (kidding): How about your breasts? Would you show them?
Sharleen: I'd show them. You like my breasts; you know I've got the finest pink nipples you've ever laid your eyes on.

[*Sharleen smiles at Cruiser*]

Cruiser: It's true.

[*Cruiser laughs*]

Sharleen: I'll show you my nipples.

[*She starts to unbutton her blouse, but stops*]

Cruiser: I'd do anything for ya!
Sharleen: Anything?

He grabs her around the neck and pulls her toward him. His hand works its way under her blouse.

Cruiser: Let's get it on! You want me? C'mon.
Sharleen: Do you have any food? I'm hungry. Let's eat first.

He goes to a small icebox and takes out some food. Sharleen sits on the table and eats; she touches his face.

Sharleen: Go shave.
Cruiser: Forget it!
  [*He comes behind her, unbuttons her blouse, and pulls it off*]
Sharleen: Hey! You're too much! You ripped my shirt!
Cruiser: I want you.
Sharleen: C'mon now, easy.
Cruiser: You're afraid!
Sharleen (laughing): Afraid of what? You?

He lifts her up to him, carries her to the couch, and lays her on her back.

Sharleen: You like me?
Cruiser: You feel good.
Sharleen: It's good for me too.
   [*She kisses him full on the mouth; Cruiser moves on top of her*]
Sharleen (sullen): No, not now!
   [*She pushes him off and she stands*]
Sharleen: I'll come back tomorrow night!
Cruiser: What's wrong?

Sharleen: I'm having my thing.
Cruiser: Shut up and get out!
Sharleen: You're crazy!
       [*Cruiser hits the wall with his fist*]

Act IV

Scene i. *Line cabin*

Expecting Dax *to return momentarily,* Billy *reads. Everything is quiet except for the crackling of the fire. Suddenly the revving of an engine disturbs the silence. She moves to the window and sees the approaching snowmobile. Alarmed, she takes the shotgun down from above the fireplace, examines the chambers, and removes the safety. Placing the gun on top of the table, she quickly goes through the cabinets and finds a box of shells, then carefully loads the shotgun. She opens the door.*

Cruiser *kills the snowmobile engine, gets to his feet, and starts through the knee-deep snow.*

Billy: That's far enough. What do you want?
Cruiser: Thought I'd try and make it right between you and me. Ma told me you was here; thought I'd surprise you.
Billy: You're not welcome here.
Cruiser (angry): I'm cold as shit; c'mon, just let me come in and warm my hands and feet; they're frozen solid.

He continues to wade through the snow. Billy *points the shotgun at him.*

Billy: Don't make me tell you again.
Cruiser: Ah, c'mon, little sister, you can't turn your brother away in this kind of weather.

She shoots over his head, knocking herself backwards from the recoil. Cruiser *stops in his tracks.*

Billy: Get your ass out of here or you won't be so lucky next time.
Cruiser: Pull the trigger.

[*He continues forward*]

Cruiser: I'll be nice to you. Just let me come by that fire. C'mon, you sweet thing.

Billy *lets him have it with the other barrel, hitting him squarely in his right shoulder, sending him reeling backwards into the snow. In disbelief, he grasps at his bloodied shoulder.*

Cruiser: You son-of-a-bitch, cunt!
Billy: Now, get out!
 [*He gets to his feet and struggles back to the snowmobile*]
Cruiser: I'll get even.

Tucking his wounded arm close to his side, he starts the snowmobile and slowly wheels it around and moves off. Billy waits until the revving fades, then goes inside. She throws the bolt, securely locking the heavy door. Drained by emotions, she sinks down on the couch with the shotgun beside her.

 A knock at the door.

Dax: It's me, open up.
 [*She throws open the dead bolt*]
Dax: I was worried about you. What were those shots about?
Billy: Cruiser was here.
Dax: ALONE?
Billy (dazed): He was alone.
Dax: What happened?
Billy: I shot him! I told him to get out. He wouldn't listen. I shot him.
Dax: Where's he now?
Billy: Gone back, I guess.

Suddenly an ax comes crashing through the window, and Cruiser *crawls through the broken glass.* Dax *sizes him up.*

Cruiser: C'mon hit me. I'll kill ya.
 [*Dax hits him, but Cruiser doesn't flinch*]
 You yellow gutless . . .

[*Billy goes for the shotgun*]
Leave it alone, kid. I don't mean *no* harm.
{*He hits her and knocks her down*]
You harlot!

She grabs him around the ankle, and he kicks her loose. Dax *recklessly charges, butting his head into* Cruiser's *midsection, momentarily knocking the wind out of him.*

Seizing the shotgun Dax *lets go with both barrels over his head.* Cruiser's *face catches some of the shot, temporarily blinding him. Shocked, he staggers through the door back to his snowmobile.*

Struggling to remain seated on the snowmobile, Cruiser *speeds across the white fields. The full moon helps light his way, but having only one good eye, he has trouble discerning his way through the shadows.*

Suddenly, he hits a ditch and the machine comes to a dead stop. His wounded shoulder crushes the windshield and breaks part of the steering wheel. He groans in agony. Realizing how desperate his situation has become, he uses the last of his strength to try and free the machine.

A Wolf *appears in the shadows of the trees, curiously studying him. The* Wolf *howls and other* Wolves *begin appearing between the trees. The animals begin to stalk him. Sensing their approach,* Cruiser *gathers the broken plastic steering wheel for protection. The* Lead Wolf *begins to run and the others follow. The* Lead Wolf *smashes through the snow, knocking* Cruiser *backwards and sinks his fangs deep into his hand.* Cruiser *catches the* Wolf *with his fist across the snout and eye. The animal howls in agony.*

Another Wolf *bites into his thigh, and* Cruiser *crushes his skull with the broken steering wheel. Five* Wolves *hit him at once.* Cruiser's *heart pounds as the animals pull at him. His struggle grows weak, and his screams fade into the cold silence. The wind begins to blow hard as the* Wolves *tear the flesh from his bones.*

Scene ii.

Riding a snowmobile, Uncle Bud *searches the open rangeland for cattle and he spots what appears to be a downed animal being picked over by* Wolves. *As he approaches, the* Wolves *scatter. Recognizing the indistinguishable remains to be human, he wraps the frozen corpse into a blanket and ties it to the back of his machine. He retraces the tracks of the snowmobile toward the line cabin. The door is open; the cabin empty!*

Later that same day Bud *has arrived at the* Sheriff's *office with* Cruiser's *body. The* Sheriff *pulls back the blanket and exposes the corpse.*

Sheriff: Who could it be?
Bud: Damned if I know.

The Sheriff *covers the body and goes to his desk. He pulls a bottle out from inside the drawer and pours* Bud *and himself a shot.*

Sheriff: I better get the coroner in here so he can identify the body. Those wolves picked it pretty clean.
                                                          [*They drink*]
    Why don't *you* come clean with me?
Bud: What the hell you getting at?
Sheriff: You got some idea and you ain't talking, Bud! Where did you find the body?
Bud: It appears to be an accident, Sheriff. You know I ain't got nothing to hide.
Sheriff: I don't need this shit; probably some drifter got what's coming to him.

Scene iii. *Ranch house*

Bud, Dax *and* Billy *sit at the kitchen table.*

Dax: How did they figure out it was Cruiser?

Bud: Dental records, I guess.

Dax: It was my fault!

Bud: No, the wolves did it! If you had, he never would have gotten away from the cabin. You did what you needed in self-defense.

[*Billy cries. . . .*]

You got to handle it, Billy.

Billy: I'm half-crazy in my head.

Bud: Both of you stop. Sometimes a person really does have to do what you have to do. And there is no way to explain it and there is no way to justify it; you have to accept it no matter how painful. Everything is all right.

Cruiser got what was coming to him; it's the law of nature!

Billy: I need to get out of here. Please, I've got to go!

Bud: Are you sure you know what you're doing, Billy? They are reporting the temperatures to drop to forty below zero.

Billy: How long will it take to get to Wyoming?

Bud: Couple of hours, if you don't break down!

She pulls her wool cap down low on her forehead and over her ears.

Billy: Damn.

Outside the window the moon breaks out from beneath a cloud and creates a frozen blue landscape.

Billy: What's gonna happen?

Bud: Sheriff figures it's death by natural causes.

Dax: I'm not running. I came here looking for something and I found it, Bud. What you said is true, there is a right and a wrong; if you mess around with somebody, somebody's going to mess around with you.

[*He wraps his arm around Billy's neck*]

Cruiser got what was coming to him; he went too far

and nature took care of him. You're right about something else, Bud. It'll be a lucky man that ends up with you, Billy Blue.

[*Billy smiles and kisses him softly*]

Shattered Time

List of Characters

Hellman, a doctor (debarred)
Buck, the doctor's son
Cris, Buck's friend
Gayla, Buck's girlfriend
Coach
Melissa, Cris's girlfriend
Young man
Young woman
Butch, classmate
Donkey, classmate
Fat kid
Doctor
Nurse
Bartender
Oldtimers
Pitcher
Umpire

Act I

Scene i. *The vast high desert wasteland of Southern Wyoming*

A once-prosperous oil-shale town gone bust, downtown businesses have shut down because of hard times. Off Main Street, in a bleak neighborhood, a maudlin brown house appears. Inside, Hellman, *a tall, overweight doctor in his midfifties, sits at kitchen table, sipping his coffee. His son* Buck *has just returned home.*

Hellman: I saw Cris yesterday, he said he'd stop by. Told me to tell you not to make any plans for Saturday night. A lot of your old friends ask about you; your baseball coach thinks you're the greatest. He still can't get over that game you pitched in the State Championship.

[*Buck smiles*]

Buck (remembering): Good ole coach.

Hellman: He thinks you could have made it to the major leagues, if you'd put your mind to it. Hell, boy, you have to think about settling down. Make something of yourself. You're living on easy street. It'll catch up to you. Look at me! I've worked my fingers to the bone.

Buck: There's just no work for me around here. Mom worked hard, what did she have to show for it?

Hellman: All she wanted to do was travel. She had a wild streak in her. She was just like you. Nowadays, all you kids just hang around and watch TV. When I was growing up life was hard, there was no time for foolin' around. My ole man would have knocked me sideways if I had talked to him about the crap you talk about.

It's not too late to go back to the University. I'm sure that baseball scholarship is still good. You'd be fixed for the rest of your life.

Someone KNOCKS at the back door. Cris, Buck's *high school buddy, enters.*

Cris: Hello, Doc.
Hellman: Cris!
[*Buck stands and warmly greets his friend*]
Cris: Dang! It's really you. Back from the big city!
[*They square off and fake punches at each other*]
Buck: What's new? You and Sally still going together?
Cris: We broke up over a year ago. You remember!
Buck: Oh, yeah!
Cris: I'm going steady with Melissa. We're getting married!
[*Buck tries to act interested*]
Buck: Oh, that's great!
Cris: You broke her heart when you left. But she fell for me like a lead weight.
Buck: Right!
[*Buck winks!*]
Cris: Everybody's asking about you. Remember your old flame, Stephanie? She's a movie star now and Jimmy B, he's in the slammer, but you'll get all the gossip tonight at the high school reunion. I bet you can't wait to see everybody again.

Remember when you were voted the most likely to succeed?
[*He looks at the kitchen clock*]
Gotta run, promised I'd pick up Melissa. Nice to see you again, Doc.
Hellman: Same here, Cris. Tell your folks hi for me.
Cris: Sure thing. (*to Buck*) I'll pick you up at eight.
[*Cris leaves*]
Hellman: Cris looks good. He tells me his father is selling a lot of insurance policies. ONE thing people need these days is *insurance.*

He absentmindedly daydreams. Buck *goes to the window and watches* Cris *drive off.*

Hellman: I remember when I took your mother to my tenth high school reunion; that was a dance I'll never forget. I was fresh out of medical school and your ma and I had been dating about three months. She enjoyed dancing and I thought it would be a good chance for her to meet some of my old friends. What I didn't figure was the way they treated her because she was part *Indian.* My friends said she belonged on a reservation. I couldn't believe my ears; they called her a squaw! That night I damn near got into a fist fight. I thought people would accept her once we got married, but your ma always felt that people talked about her behind her back. She'd get these terrible headaches, worried sick over gossip. I'd tell her she was imagining things. She didn't deserve the way they treated her.

Buck *starts into the living room; pictures of his mother are scattered over the walls, he lies out on the couch and switches a football game on TV.* Buck *silently watches*

Buck: Seems like someday they'll be playing football year around. I don't know how those guys can take that kinda punishment.
Hellman: If you made their money, it wouldn't matter how many times you got hit.
Buck: Half those guys can't even walk after they turn forty years old. I got more respect for my body!
Hellman: You ain't making that kinda money, *BUDDY!*
Buck: Just because there's money in something doesn't mean it's right!
Hellman: What kind of work were you doing in Salt Lake City?
Buck: Working construction.
Hellman: I didn't think you knew anything about construction.
Buck: It doesn't take much know-how to pound nails.
   [*Buck changes TV stations with the remote control*]
Hellman: I wish you worked in town so I might see more of you.

[*His mind drifts*]
Sometimes I wonder why your mother had to die so young. It doesn't seem fair, a woman healthy and strong. . . . Then one day she gets a brain tumor. She always had that need to wander. When we first married, she wanted to travel to the Southwest and look for a lost Indian civilization. Boy, she was a daydreamer.
[*He takes up his journal*]
Buck: Why didn't you go?
Hellman: I had responsibilities; you were just six months old, it would have been too foolish running off with a newborn.
[*Hellman puts his journal down*]
She was born a century late. Folks around here could never see the beauty she had within; they only saw her brown skin and her Indian heritage.
[*Hellman gets sad and moody. Buck turns off the TV*]
Buck: Oh, I miss her.
[*He wipes away a tear*]
Hellman: You were her pride and joy. She always thought you'd make something of yourself. She'd say, now you watch Buck, he'll make it big! Probably get a job at the bank, something respectable.
Buck: Please.
[*Buck takes his mother's picture off the wall and studies it*]
I remember how I found her dead, clutching that arrowhead. She always thought that piece of stone would protect her when her time came.
Hellman: STOP IT! I don't want to talk about it.
Buck: She had that terrible distorted face, like she'd seen the devil and he took her spirit.

Hellman *snatches the picture from* Buck; *it falls to the floor, breaking the glass.* Buck *wanders to the window and looks out on the bleak Wyoming landscape.*

Scene ii. *High school auditorium*

A high school reunion is in progress. Couples come and go between the dance and parking lot. Buck and Cris drink beer beside Cris's car.

Cris: Dang that Melissa, the way she warms up when Charlie Stacker comes around. The thing is he knows well enough that she's my girl!
   [*He squeezes his beer can flat and pops open another*]
Buck: She's always been that way, Cris. You overlook what you don't want to see. She was the same way when I went out with her.
   [*They drink*]
Cris: I suppose she'll change once we get married.

Silhouetted by the auditorium lights, Melissa, high school beauty queen, fresh and sassy, comes out of auditorium flirting with Charlie. Melissa breaks away from Charlie's embrace and starts toward them. Cris guzzles his beer as she approaches.

Melissa (to Buck): Well, I'll be. So it's true. King Jock returns. Ain't we privileged!
Cris: C'mon, Melissa, lay off.
Melissa: Break any hearts lately?
Buck: Hello, Melissa.

She ignores him and climbs into Cris's car and fixes her makeup.

Cris: Sorry about that.
Buck: Glad she's not my PROBLEM any more.

Cris gets into the car besides Melissa, and they get into a heated argument.

Cris: What the hell's going on between you and Charlie?
   [*Melissa continues to look in the mirror*]
   C'mon now. I got eyes.

[*Buck ambles off toward dance*]

Standing beside the front door, Coach, *stocky, balding fifties, drinks a Coke. The* Band *plays bobby socks music and the gym floor is crowded with* Couples. Buck *enters.*

Coach: Well, I'll be hog-tied! Aren't you a sight for sore eyes. Doc told me you'd be back! How's it going?

[*They shake*]

Buck: Hello, Coach.
Coach: How's the arm? Been throwing lately?
Buck: Naw!
Coach: Man, I wish I'd had you pitching on the team this last year. We never made it to the finals. Rock Springs beat us in the first round, not even close. I don't have anybody who can throw the ball.
Buck: How about Rink?
Coach: He threw his arm out. There's this sophomore kid who could be good, but he's too short.

[*Coach burps*]

How'd you like to be my assistant? You could show these kids what it takes. Man, you had a great curve, let's see that wind-up.

[*Coach winds up*]

Buck: C'mon, Coach, not now.
Coach: Man, you could have made it *BIG time.*

Remember when the scouts came up from Kansas City to watch you pitch. They were ready to sign you up, but your ma wouldn't hear of it.
Buck: I was only a junior. Besides, I wasn't ready.
Coach: Didn't matter! They would have trained you, put you on one of their farm teams; you had the best arm of any kid I ever coached.

[*Couple step off the dance floor and approach*]

Young Man: Hold it! Look who's here!

[*Young man eagerly shakes hands with Buck*]

I told you he'd be back.
Young Woman: You sure look good, Buck. How have things been going?

Buck: Good! Good to see you both together again.

[*Couple leaves. Cris enters in emotional state*]

Cris: Melissa's gone. She gave me my ring back. She's calling everything off.

[*Coach eavesdrops on conversation*]

We had a big fight.

Buck: You want to talk about it?

Buck *puts his arm on* Cris's *shoulder, and they wander toward the refreshments.*

Buck: See you later, Coach.
Coach: Think about that job offer.

As they move through the crowd Buck is stopped time and again to shake hands with schoolmates he hasn't seen over the past year. He receives warm welcomes as a returning hero, a high school legend. Donkey, a depressed Hispanic, approaches.

Buck: How's the back, Donkey? You still collecting workmen's comp?

[*Donkey stretches*]

Donkey: As long as they keep paying, I'm not complaining.
Cris: Have you been looking for work, or just collecting money?

[*Donkey laughs*]

Donkey: The state of Wyoming's taking good care of me. You guys having a good time?

[*Donkey spots a girl in the corner*]

Man, she's got the tits! You've got to move fast; the good ones get picked up like that.

[*He snaps his fingers*]

Personally, I think women are good for one thing. If you boys will excuse me.

[*He leaves; they move through the crowd*]

Cris: Can you believe Donkey, still drawing workmen's compensation from an injury two years ago. Sometimes ya gotta wonder. Do you think he's sandbagging?

Buck: He *was* hurt pretty bad; spent six months in physical therapy, remember?

Cris: He's always feeling sorry for himself; he's moody. I think he's on some kinda drug for depression. All he does all day is hang around looking at TV. I'd go crazy. Why doesn't he get a job?

[*Cris and Buck approach Butch at the punch bowl*]

Butch: Can I get you girls a beer?

Buck: I'm dry as a bone.

Butch: Bartender, two beers for the girls.

[*He drinks what's left in his glass*]

So, when did you get home?

Buck: This morning.

[*Chaperone pours three punches*]

Butch: Well, you ready to make some real money?

Buck: I could use some money. Sure thing.

[*He fumbles with his glass*]

That last job I had stunk! But I got too many bills to pay off and nothing left in the bank.

Butch: Stop your moaning. I just signed a *BIG CONTRACT* to frame a house on *SNOB* Hill. I gotta finish the job by December one.

[*They drink*]

I need you to help pound nails.

Buck: No problem!

Butch: I've heard that before! (*pause*) Why did you come home?

Buck: I guess I felt guilty about my dad being alone. Besides, I had enough of Salt Lake City.

Butch: Every time I go home, I can't wait to leave. My ole man gets on my butt about everything *AND ANYTHING!*

Cris: Personally, I'd give anything to get out of *this* town. Ain't Sal got the life with that place of his on Maui. I wouldn't mind that warm weather right about now.

[*They drink*]

Butch: Hey, listen, I got a six pack and a bottle of Southern Comfort in the truck. Let's go get drunk. Whaddaya say!

Cris: Sounds good to me.

Buck: Maybe some other time.

He leaves Cris *and* Butch *and goes outside.*

A hippie van painted in rainbow designs pulls into the parking lot and flashes its lights, temporarily blinding him. Gayla, an Indian girl, opens the door and starts toward him, her dress flowing in the night air.

Gayla: I thought you'd be here.
Buck: I'm glad to see you again.
Gayla: You have enough of the dance?

Buck *pulls her close and tries to kiss her, but she moves back.*

Buck: What's wrong?

He follows her behind her van. She wraps her arms around his neck and they start to make out.

Buck: This is crazy, trying to fool everybody.
Gayla: It's the only way.

Fat Kid *wanders through parking lot and gives* Gayla *a hard look, as if to say "We don't like Indians around here."*

Buck: Something wrong?
Fat Kid: Who's the squaw?
Buck: You got a lot of nerve, *fatass*. Get out of here!
[*Fat kid runs off*]
Gayla: What's wrong?
Buck: Doesn't it make you feel weird?
Gayla: It's not the first time someone called me a squaw.
Buck: This is crazy trying to hide from everyone.
Gayla: It's the only way, your father would never allow it! You know how he feels.
Buck: I'll tell him.
Gayla: Please, let's wait. You just got home, we have plenty of time.
[*They walk*]
Did you really miss me, or are you just saying that?
[*He stops*]

Buck: I didn't know how much I felt for you until I was gone.
[*He pulls her close*]
   I love you.

Scene iii. *A new house in the framing process*

Buck *and* Cris*'s breath freezes as they pound nails.* Butch *approaches carrying coffee and a box of donuts.*

Butch: Let's take a break.

Buck *and* Cris *take off their carpenter's belts and huddle together next to a fire as* Butch *passes out the coffee and donuts.*

Buck: Thanks, Butch. You're a real Buckeroo.
[*They drink their coffee*]
Cris: I can't believe how cold it is.
[*Butch chews his sweetroll*]
Butch: Boy, I'll be glad once we get a roof on this place.
[*Butch studies the half-framed structure*]
Buck: Do you think I could get a little draw on wages?
Butch: What's the problem?
Buck: How about two hundred?
Butch: I'll see what I can do.
   [*A blast of WIND forces them to draw closer to the fire*]
   Now, let's stop the B.S., and get this place done before the snow flies.

Cris *and* Buck *reluctantly put on their carpenter's belts and go back to pounding nails.* Cris *takes measurements and calls out the lengths of boards to be cut to* Buck, *who works the chop saw.*

Cris: Thirty-two and three quarters, thirty-three, thirty-two and a half.
   [*Buck cuts madly, but gets confused and has to remeasure*]
      Thirty-one.

[*Buck, impatient, fumbles with tape measure*]
You said you wanted to cut, but last time you measured everything wrong.

[*Buck scratches his head*]

Buck: Okay, okay, just give me a break!

He makes several cuts and brings the blocks to Cris. Cris *tries fitting the blocks between the framed studs, but nothing fits.*

Cris: Everything is either too long or too short. What are you doing?

Buck: The chop saw must be off!

Cris: Impossible.

[*Buck starts to remeasure the blocks and Cris notices his broken tape measure*]

Cris: Let me see that thing.

[*He grabs Buck's tape measure and examines it. The end of the tape is broken and missing the first inch*]
What is this?

Buck: Nobody's perfect. Its a little broken. You're too serious, you need to learn how to relax.

[*Cris pulls another tape out of his belt and gives it to Buck*]

Cris: Use this and get rid of that piece of junk!

[*Buck tosses the broken tape high into the air, catches it behind his back and puts it into his belt*]

Cris: It's about quitting time, let's pick up.

They take off their belts and sweep up. Butch *approaches with paychecks.*

Butch: You guys get anything done this afternoon?

[*He passes out the paychecks, Buck is delighted to see that Butch has advanced him two hundred dollars*]

Buck: Alright, thanks for the draw! You're a pal.

Butch: Just make sure you're back here Monday morning, eight o'clock sharp. No more of the eight-thirty business.

Buck: Whatever you say, Boss.

[*He throws his carpenter's belt over his shoulder and starts for his truck*]

See you girls later.

[*He gets into the truck and drives off*]

Scene iv. Gayla *sits beside* Buck *as he drives his truck. They enter the national park and the landscape becomes incomprehensible as the setting sun creates imaginary images on the red rocks.*

As the last rays of light begin to fade they enter a box canyon.

Buck: I've never seen anything like it! How did you ever find this place?

Gayla: Wait till you see it in daylight. Pull over and park by the big trees. We'll set up there.

[*He parks the truck*]

Buck: This is unbelievable. It's magic! (*pause*) I had no idea it was going to be like this.

They unload their camping gear out of the back of the pickup and set up camp. The air begins to cool down as the sun drops below the ridge.

Dressed in heavy jackets, wool caps, and gloves, Buck *feeds the fire with dried kindling as* Gayla *opens a can of chili and pours it into a pot.*

Gayla: I think the temperature has dropped thirty degrees since we got here.

[*Buck takes a deep breath*]

Buck: Man, this air smells good.

Gayla *puts the pot over the open fire then takes a flask out of a box. She passes the flask to* Buck, *who gulps down the whiskey. He wipes his chin with his glove and raises the flask.*

Buck: Here's to being alive!

[*He drinks*]

Being here stirs something in my blood. It feels good!

Gayla *gets two tin plates and scoops the chili out of the pot. They sit beside the campfire and eat.*

Buck: I don't know where I fit in anymore! I wish I could just go along with things, instead I'm always searching. (*pause*) It's confusing when people keep telling you what they think you should be. I'm tired of feeling guilty about what others expect of me. (*pause*) My father acts like I'm still a child.
Gayla: Why don't you tell him how you feel?
Buck: You don't know my father. He thinks he's got all the answers, and besides, maybe my ole man's right, maybe I don't have any ambition. Look at the guys I hang out with, all Butch and Donkey care about is getting drunk.
Gayla: I wish I knew what went on inside that head of yours.
Buck: I guess I'm afraid of love.
Gayla: Because I'm Navajo?

[*Buck looks away*]

Buck: I felt so resentful of the way people treated my mother.
Gayla: Try not to worry, everything will be all right.

Buck *takes a small box out of his pocket, opens it and hands her a ring.*

Buck: I never want to lose you.

[*He holds her tight then kisses her*]

Gayla: Stop worrying, I love you.

[*She smiles and cozies up to him*]

You're cute.

[*She touches his face and draws close, kissing him on the lips*]

I can see I'll have to teach you how to kiss again.

[*He laughs*]

Now relax and let me do the kissing.

[*She kisses him*]

Much better. Let's try again.

Act II

Scene i. *Covered with climbing ropes and pitons,* Buck *and* Gayla *scale the face of a rock wall like spiders. The meandering Lost River lies a thousand feet below as they balance precariously on tiny ledges.*

Buck (calling back to Gayla): C'mon, it's easy.
Gayla: I don't know how I let you talk me into this!

Buck *continues to climb and reaches the summit.*

Buck (calling out): You should see the view from the top.

Gayla's *face appears, then crawling on hands and knees she approaches.*

Buck: Doesn't it make you feel good to know you climbed that, just you and the mountain, hand in hand? Don't you get a shot of energy from being so close to nature?
[*Gayla lies on the ground totally exhausted as Buck absorbs the scenery*]
Gayla: You'd probably keep going until you dropped. I'm happy just looking at these mountains. That's the difference between us, you've got to experience things to an extreme.
Buck: Don't you like to challenge yourself?
Gayla: Not everyone is quite as brave as you!
Buck: Let's go, c'mon.

They hike up a narrow trail toward El Dorado, a steep rock face.
   Buck *starts up the tragic rock. Every fifteen feet he stops and hammers pitons into the black mass then runs his rope through the steel protection and tests its hold. Satisfied, he continues up.*

His movement slows immensely at the complexity of the climb. At one point, he waits five minutes to make a change in hand holds.

Gayla: You okay?
Buck: It's tricky.

Somehow he realizes he's in above his head, but at this point in the climb there's no turning back; he must go on.

Indian paintings appear on the rock as he blindly feels for a foothold.

He moves ahead and the rock falls away beneath his foot sending him backwards into midair over the top of Gayla. *The lead protection pulls out of the rock, flipping him head-first towards the bottom.*

Gayla *screams. Somehow, her protection holds, but* Buck *is helplessly spinning and twisting in midair. He lands on his head, splitting open his skull.*

Gayla *quickly moves down the rock towards his motionless body. By the time she reaches him, he has gone into convulsions and has stopped breathing. She tries artificial respiration and slowly he starts to breathe again. Blood oozes out of his fractured skull. Overwhelmed by her situation* Gayla *screams.*

Gayla: Help!
                      [*The words echo off the rock walls*]
    Help!

Again the word echoes back at her. She holds Buck *in her arms and her emotions give way. Blood from the open wound covers her shirt.*

Gayla: Please! I need help.

She uses strips of cloth out of her pack to bandage the wound and stop the bleeding.

She begins to collect fallen branches that are scattered about and, using her climbing ropes, she binds the branches together and builds a lean-to type stretcher. Carefully, she rolls Buck *onto the stretcher. Using additional ropes she builds a harness and secures it around her waist, and starts down the trail.*

Scene ii. *A hospital waiting room*

Hellman *and* Doctor *are in heated conversation over* Buck's *condition.*

Hellman: You had no right to operate on him without my consent. He's not a ward of the state!
Doctor: His trachea was blocked and he stopped breathing; he could have died. I tried to reach you, but there was no answer!
    He's still in a coma; we are doing tests on him right now. I expect we'll know the results shortly.
    [*Hellman stands, his face remains blank of emotion*]
Hellman: Keep me posted of his progress. I don't expect my son to become some guinea pig.
Doctor: My God, what are you saying? You were a doctor once, before they pulled your license for unethical practice.
Hellman: I know what can happen to coma victims; they can be kept alive weeks, months, years without making any progress.
    [*He stomps past Gayla, then stops*]
    You Indian bitch, leave my son alone; if it wasn't for you, none of this would have happened!
Gayla: Please.
Hellman: Stay away!
    [*He leaves*]

Exhausted from her vigil, Gayla *slips into a seat.* Cris *enters.*

Gayla: Oh, Cris, this has been such a nightmare.
Cris: Has me made any progress?
    [*Gayla nods her head*]

Gayla: It was a freak accident, it wasn't anyone's fault!

[*Gayla breaks down and cries*]

Gayla (sobbing): It's been so awful. I feel so helpless. They don't give him much of a chance to live.

Cris: He's strong, he'll make it!

[*Doctor enters*]

Gayla: Where is he? I want to see him. Please, I want to see him.

Doctor: If you want, follow me.

They follow the Doctor *into intensive care. A* Nurse *sits beside a monitor. X rays of* Buck's *fractured skull hang on the wall.* Buck *lies in bed, covered with tubes; his skull is bandaged and bloody.* Gayla *moves beside him, she touches his face and begins to cry. His body remains motionless.*

Cris (whispering): Buck . . . Buck . . . It's Cris.

[*Buck opens his eyes*]

Cris: It's me . . . Cris. Can you hear me, Buck?

[*He blinks*]

Cris (to Gayla): I think he hears me.

[*Gayla moves closer*]

Cris: Buck, blink if you can hear me.

[*He blinks*]

Cris: Buck, you had a climbing accident. You're in the hospital.

Gayla (to Cris): Talk to him again.

Cris: Blink if you can hear me, Buck.

[*Buck blinks, but is exhausted from the effort*]

Nurse: Let's leave him alone. He needs rest.

Cris: Can you hear me, Buck?

[*Buck nods. Cris reaches for his hand*]

Cris: Squeeze my hand.

[*Buck squeezes his hand*]

Cris: Good.

[*A distorted smile crosses Buck's face*]

Cris: Hang in there. You're going to be okay.

[*Buck moans out Cris's name*]

Buck: C-R-I-S!

[*His lips create a distorted smile*]

Gayla: Hello, Buck.

[*He reaches for her, but his hand drops from exhaustion*]

Nurse: Let him rest.

[*Reluctantly, they leave*]

Scene iii. *High school auditorium*

A banner hangs above the high school stage, reading, "Buck's Benefit." The school band plays in the background. As friends fill the auditorium, Hellman *and* Coach *talk.*

Hellman: Ever since he was a little boy, he's had a mind of his own. He could have been a professional baseball pitcher if he stuck with it, but he couldn't handle what it took to make the BIG LEAGUE. Let me tell you something. I know he could have been the BEST. I had to push Buck. I always wanted him to be a WINNER.

Coach: Life's competition. If you can't compete, you're a LOSER.

Hellman: My wife would sit and listen to the birds all day if she could. Daydreamer, just like Buck. Problem with young people today, they're lazy, afraid of hard work.

Coach: You gotta push these kids.

Hellman: I use to be real busy with my medical practice; then some asshole complains and they jerk my license for no reason. I don't know what the hell this world is coming to.

Once I thought I had all the answers; now it's like I'm drifting day by day. I suppose you know what that's all about?

Coach: What the hell do you mean by that comment?

[*Hellman ignores him*]

Hellman: I remember all the suffering my wife went through before she died. Sometimes I think she didn't need to be kept alive to suffer the way she did.

Coach: Buck told me what happened. I'm sorry.
> I've almost reached the point. . . .

Coach: What?

Hellman: You ever feel like you're living on the edge of *nowhere?*

Coach: You need to take up a sport! I'm into hunting myself. Nothing like a good kill to stop thinking. Have you ever tried to stop thinking?

Hellman: You're talking bullshit.

Coach *moves off, leaving* Hellman *standing alone.* Cris *climbs on stage, ready to begin the auction.*

Cris: Let me have your attention, please.
> [*Friends quiet*]
> You all know why we're here. Every dollar we raise will go to help pay medical bills for Buck, so be generous. The first item is a season pass at Yellowstone. What do I hear?

First Friend: One hundred

Second Friend: One hundred fifty.

Third Friend: Three hundred.

Cris: SOLD!

Auction continues in background, Hellman *goes outside. Alone beneath the moon,* Hellman *talks to the universe.*

Hellman: Damn. Buck, why did you have to go and make such a mess of things? Your mother's not going to let me rest until I'm undone. She's come back as your Indian girl.
> [*He lowers his head*]
> I'm damned.

Scene iv. *Buck's hospital room*

Buck *appears to be resting peacefully as* Cris *enters and moves close behind his semi-conscious friend.*

Cris: Hello, Buck.

[*Buck opens his eyes*]

Cris: How we doing?

[*Buck's eyes widen*]

Buck: Get me out of H-E-R-E!
Cris: Easy partner, you took a bad fall.
Buck: I'm tired of all the tests and medications they're trying on me. Get me out of here!
Cris: You're still weak, be patient. When the time is right, we'll get you out!
Buck: I need to smell some flowers, I'm living in hell. There's nothing here but the smell of death!
Cris: You're talking crazy! Stop, it only makes the situation harder to handle.

[*Buck's eyes transmit a powerful message*]

Buck: Get me OUT!
Nurse *enters and becomes alarmed by* Buck's *emotional state.*

Nurse: Please, Son, you'll have to leave.
[*Tear swell in Buck's eyes as his friend departs his bedside*]
Buck: O-U-T!

[*Nurse tries to calm Buck as Cris leaves the room*]

Hospital—Later that night
The hospital appears to be empty except for an occasional Nurse *coming and going.* Cris *and* Gayla *silently move down the hallway, avoiding detection. They slither around corners and finally enter* Buck's *room.*

Buck: Gayla!

[*She embraces him*]

Cris: Listen to me Buck. We're going to see if you can walk, but we have to be quiet as possible.

[*His eyes light up and he nods his approval*]

They get Buck *to his feet, drape his arms over their shoulders, and together they make their way across the room. His movements are painful at first.*

Cris: Easy now.

Buck's muscles relax and he begins to walk. After several passes, they lower him to a chair.

Chris: How'd that feel?

[*Buck smiles wide*]

Buck: Again!

They lift him as before and start across the room.

Buck: I feel lucky to have you as friends.
Cris: Man, you got courage.
Buck: I was afraid when I was hooked up to those tubes, not knowing my name or how to speak. I couldn't remember a thing. I was scared, believe me.
Cris: One thing does puzzle me. It's your dad; he's a mysterious guy. He's been wandering around dead drunk since your accident. Is it safe for you to go back home?
Buck: I'll be okay. He's got a lot of feelings bottled up inside. He's just a lonely man. (*pause*) Just get me out of this hospital!

Act III

Scene i. *Hellman's house*

Buck *has been released from the hospital and is convalescing at home. He rests on the couch.* Cris *sits beside him.*

Buck: I thought he'd be happy to see me out of the hospital, but he acts annoyed that I'm alive. I don't understand.

All my life I have tried to please him, but he acts so dissatisfied and frustrated with me. When I came out of the coma, I had a lot of time to think. All my life I have wanted to please him.

Baseball, that was for him; the better I did the more he'd expect, the more he expected the harder I'd play. I couldn't play hard enough; he'd always expect more! After my mother died, I couldn't face him anymore. He drove me away. I had to leave my friends and Gayla.

The day I fell off the rock. I could feel all his anger.

[*The sound of a revving engine can be heard, then quiet*]

Buck: The return of Dr. Jekyll.

Hellman (off stage) (yelling): Buck, you *shit*! I've come back!

Suddenly the door swings open and Hellman *appears, slobbering drunk, looking like a madman. A look of terror crosses Buck's face.*

Hellman: Where is that little son-of-a-bitch kid of mine!

Hellman *stumbles into the room, letting the door slam behind him. The dim light reveals the frightening figure of a man driven to the brink of insanity.*

Hellman *(yelling):* Buck!

Hellman *sways wildly into the darkness and falls face first to the floor, knocking himself out.* Cris, *shocked by* Hellman's *behavior, sits dumbfounded.*

Cris: What's got into him?
      [Cris *moves over* Hellman, *who has begun to snore*]
Buck: You better go.
      [Cris *leaves*]

Hellman *regains consciousness and throws up. Weak and ashamed, he sits holding his head.* Buck *observes his behavior.* Hellman *looks straight ahead.*

Buck: What happened? You seem pretty angry about something. Anything you want to talk about?
Hellman: I got drunk, drunk as I've ever been.
Buck: You frightened me.
Hellman: You don't know what I've been through this last year. I get these terrible headaches that last fifteen, twenty minutes. Feels like my brain wants to explode.
      [*He holds his head*]
    The whole damn thing is sinful. Everyone in town knows you're sleeping with that squaw.
Buck: How can you say that after all she has done for me? I'm sick of your hypocrisy.
Hellman: I know what's going to happen when you and her try and make a life together, the same thing that happened between me and your mother. People talk and eventually that talk gets to you until you can't take it anymore.
Buck: When I first met Gayla, there was something I resisted about her. Something that I felt down deep. I didn't really understand at first. It was fear of what people would say. It's so deep in my subconscious I couldn't see the love she had for me.
Hellman: Stop talking about what you don't understand.
Buck: I do understand people talking about Mom shattered your image of yourself. You were always worried about what people thought about you. You never really loved her.

Hellman: I don't like myself, never have, never will. I've always put people down to make myself feel important. I'm a son-of-a-bitch.

[*He stands*]

I ruined my marriage and drove you away from me; we're both strangers to each other.
Buck: It's not too late to work things out. We all make mistakes; you're human.
Hellman: I'm going to town. I want to be alone. My life has been one regret after another. I'm tired of living. I want to be left alone.

[*He walks out*]

Scene ii. *Saloon*

Two Old-timers *sit at the bar conversing with the* Bartender. Buck *enters and approaches them.*

Bartender: What can I do for you, partner?
Buck: I'm looking for someone.
First Old-timer: Me too, kid.

[*Second Old-timer laughs*]

Bartender: Let the boy talk, you ole fool.
Buck: The guy I'm looking for goes by the name Doc, about six four, two hundred pounds, dark hair.
First Old-timer: Sounds like my wife.
Second Old-timer: She's damn near three hundred pounds, you old fart.
Buck: Seriously, have you seen anybody who would fit that description?
Bartender: Doc came in yesterday and drank himself under the table. I threw him out. He come back again this afternoon, promised me he'd stop mouthing off. Felt sorry for him so I let him in. He's over there.

[*Buck starts for the dimly lit corner of the room*]

Dirty and unshaven, Hellman *sits alone at a green felt-covered* table, dealing himself poker hands. Buck *approaches, but* Hellman's *eyes remain fixed on his cards.*

Buck: I was worried about you.
    [*Hellman shuffles and deals a new hand; he takes three new cards*]
Hellman: Listen, kids, I've got things down deep. Just get the hell out of here.
Buck: I'm here to listen if you need to talk, but don't treat me like this. I don't deserve it!
    [*Hellman looks up from the cards and studies Buck*]
Hellman: Sit down!
    [*Buck sits; Hellman shuffles*]
    I've been carrying some excess baggage.
    [*Hellman shuffles*]
    You want to play a hand?
Buck: Sure.

Hellman *deals them each five cards. They look at their cards.*

Hellman: I need to talk about your mother.
    [*Buck studies his father*]
    How many cards do you want?
Buck: Give me two.

Hellman *deals him two cards, then takes three cards and stares* Buck *down.*

Hellman: You ever know what it's like to hurt so bad you want to puke? When your mother had that brain tumor, I died a little every day until I couldn't stand it. The doctors told me they could cure her, but I knew better. I could see the look of death in her face. I've seen it before. She just lay there and suffered day after day. . . .
    [*Hellman's eyes moisten*]
    I *killed* her. I suffocated her . . . Buck!
    [*Hellman breaks down and weeps*]
    When you had your accident, all hell broke loose in

my head, like your mother came back to revenge what I had done to her. I'm sick with guilt, like it's a cancer and it's eating at my guts. I wish I could change what is, but it's too late.

Buck: She was dying; you didn't want her to suffer. I understand how you felt; you did what you thought was right for her. You need to forget.

Hellman's eyes remain fixed on his cards. He downs the glass of whiskey beside him.

Buck: I forgive you.
Hellman: I killed her! I *killed HER!*
                                    [*The cards fall from his hands*]
    I'm leaving Evanston.
                                                [*He shuffles*]
    You'll need a place to live. You can have the house. I don't care about the Indian girl either. It doesn't matter anymore.

Buck, *anxious for his father's well-being, leans over and touches his shoulder.*

Hellman: Let me be alone. I need to sort some things out.
    I'll come back when I'm ready. We'll talk it out then.
    [*He shuffles and deals three cards face up. All queens*]
Buck: Ride back with me.
Hellman: I'll find my way back. Go ahead.
                                                 [*Buck leaves*]

Old-timers *linger outside the front door. The* Bartender *wipes down the bar and closes out the cash register.* Bartender *approaches* Hellman.

Bartender: I'm ready to close her up. Come on, let's go. Get *OUT.*
Hellman: Make us another drink.
Bartender: Get OUT!

Hellman *pulls out his revolver and cocks it.* Bartender *cautiously moves back into doorway.*

Bartender: What the hellzzz got into you?
   [*Hellman's eyes shut and he sways back into the seat*]
Bartender: Easy now, Doc. Just put down the gun and I'll let you be.

Hellman *puts the revolver on the table, and the* Bartender *wheels around, clutching his cash, and runs for the front door.* **BAM BAM BAM**. *Shots from the bar echo into the night.*

Act IV

Scene i. *Baseball field, six months later*

The Evanston Bulldogs *lead six to five in the top of the ninth inning. The* Visitors *are at the plate with three men on the bases.* Buck *coaches from the dugout.* Gayla, *seven months' pregnant, sits between* Coach *and* Cris *in the bleachers.*

Baseball Player *comes to plate.* Umpire *confers with* Visiting Coach. *Once the crowd has quieted,* Pitcher *winds up and delivers a fast ball.*

Umpire: Strike One!
Buck (shouting at Pitcher): Nice and easy, you got him.

Pitcher *nervously fingers the ball, then winds up and delivers.* Batter *hits ball solid into right field, but it goes foul.*

Umpire: Strike two!

Buck *comes out of the dugout to the edge of the playing field.*

Buck (calling out to pitcher): Easy now, Buddy.

Pitcher *kicks dirt around the mound, then delivers a wild pitch. The* Catcher *recovers the ball in the dirt, and the* Visitors *are unable to advance their bases.*

Umpire: Ball one!

Buck *starts for the mound and puts his arm around the* Pitcher's *shoulder.*

Buck: You got it in you, now. Just relax, Buddy, you can do it.
Pitcher: I *can* do it, Coach. I've got it in me!

Buck: Sure you can, Buddy, you brought us this far. Now take a couple of deep breaths and strike this *SUCKER* out!

He returns to the dugout and the Pitcher *nervously rubs the baseball with both hands. He starts a slow windup and throws a fast ball past the batter.*

Umpire: Strike threeee!

[*The hometown fans go berserk*]

Bulldogs *come off field wild with excitement; they gather around the* Pitcher *and raise him into the air.* Gayla *comes out of the grandstand and joins* Buck *on the field.*

Gayla: That was great, just great!
Buck: I learned something about myself today, Gayla. I got careless once. I paid the price. I'm happy to be alive.

All this time I thought my father was so strong, but underneath he was more sensitive than me. He probably never really understood himself until it was too late. I suppose I should feel sad, but he's probably more peaceful now he's ever been in his life.

He talked once about his heart, told me it was broken. I understand now.

The Three Captains

List of Characters

Cap, a sailor
Andy, Cap's brother
Al, Andy's friend
Peaches, Cap's ex-girlfriend
Red Diamond, the villain
Rondo, Red's goon
Knuckles, Red's goon
Karen, cocktail waitress
Violet, Caribbean woman
Como, Violet's brother
Mole, Red's sleazy pal
Bartender
Black Brothers

Act I

Scene i. *Freeport, Bahamas*

Luxurious yachts line the docks of an exclusive marina. Affluent Yachties sit on the deck overlooking their sailboats, casually letting the day slip away.

Beyond the marina, in a muddy waterway, a dilapidated, rusted yacht is tied carelessly to a dock. Liquor bottles are scattered on the deck. Faded towels and jeans hang over the safety lines.

Inside the cabin we find Cap, *unshaven and hung over as he sits at the table fumbling with his charts. Pushing everything aside, he pours himself a glass of rum. After taking a stiff drink, he turns on the radio and listens to the weather report.*

Someone knocks on the hull.

Cap: Yeah! Who is it?

As he looks out of the porthole, the companionway door opens and bright sunlight pours into the cabin. Andy, *handsome and charismatic, enters and hugs his brother.*

Andy: Hello, Cap!

Andy's overweight friend, Al, *struggles down the narrow companionway, perspiring heavily.*

Andy: You remember my old college buddy, Al?
Cap: Sure. Nice to see you again, Al.
                                        [*They shake hands*]
Andy: I can't believe it's been four years since I last saw you. Sorry I didn't get here any sooner. Mom said you needed my help!
Cap: I feel like I'm falling and there's no bottom! I'm glad you're here!
Andy: So, where are all these wild women Mom tells me about?

[Cap laughs]

Cap: C'mon, I'll show you around.

They follow him down into the main salon. Cap *turns on the stereo as* Al *sits and catches his breath. Music begins to play out of large speakers.*

Andy: It's like an old-time sailing yacht with all this teak and mahogany woodwork!
Al: I've never been on a yacht before. This is unbelievable!
Cap: The work is endless! Everything gone to hell topside!
Andy: How can you afford it?
Cap (serious): I can't! I owe the bank over one hundred thousand!
Andy: You want to talk about it!
Cap: Sure. I was making a lot of money selling real estate in Florida, closing two deals a day. We decided to start building phase four of the condo project. So, I started taking reservations. Yes, sir! I had a great future in the business. I expected to make a million dollars.

Cap *pulls out a drawing of the condo project, showing them the marina, swimming pool, tennis courts, and golf club.*

Andy: What happened?
Cap: This was the best condo project in Florida. I was making a ton of money and all it took was a signature on the dotted line!

I decided, what the hell. Why not buy a yacht? The bank loaned me the money! It was a steal at one hundred thousand, and I got the bank to finance most all of it! Payments were two thousand a month.

Then the real estate market fell apart. I couldn't close a deal. I got way behind on all my payments. A couple more big closings fell through. I gave back the Porsche, but I couldn't give up the yacht!

Then, I met this girl. Here, I'll show you her picture.

Cap *goes through his wallet and produces a picture of* Peaches, *a sexy brunette holding a tray of sandwiches.*

Andy: She's beautiful!
Al: Incredible! What's she doing?
Cap: It's a PR shot for a deli; funny you don't even notice the food.
[*Cap puts the picture back in his wallet*]
When I couldn't pay my rent, I moved in with Peaches. She helped me with my bills and fed me. We had a great thing going until she wanted to get married. She loved me, Andy!
Andy: What happened?
Cap: I split! I couldn't handle the responsibility.
Andy: Are you running?
Cap: The bank's looking for me. I haven't made a yacht payment for over six months, I'm in trouble. Thanks for coming. I feel like my brain has turned to Jello! How did I end up like this? I feel like I've aged ten years these last couple of months! Where did I go wrong?
Andy: How did you end up in the Bahamas?
Cap: After I left Florida, I sailed across the Gulf Stream. I hit a big storm and everything started to go wrong. Sails tore, halyards broke, bilge pump, radios went dead. I damn near didn't make it! I pulled in her to make repairs and ran out of money trying to fix this piece of shit! I haven't made a dime in six months. I've never been so broke in my entire life. I feel like a shithead in a gutter with my arms cut off.
Andy: I got some money, all we need to do is get this boat ready to go. Everything's going to be okay.
Al's a wizard at fixing things. Right, Al?
Al: Please, Andy, give me a break. I'm on vacation! Maybe you screwed up, Cap, but at least you're living. I'd rather be this way than doing the same job day after day!
Cap: Living? I'm living like a louse!

Scene ii. *Yacht*

Al's *hair is matted to his head as he lies in the cockpit next to* Cap, *who is wearing dirty white shorts and a stained T-shirt. The brilliant sun beats down on them.* Cap, *moaning, puts on broken sun glasses.* Al *puts his arm over his face to shade himself from the sun.*

Cap: I feel like I'm going to get sick.
Al: How did *I* end up like this?
　　　　　　　　　　[*Andy comes on deck with coffee*]
　　What happened last night?
Andy: You two finished off the rum. What do you expect!
Cap: Leave me alone!
Andy: Have some coffee. It'll help.
　　　　　　　　　　[*Cap and Al sit up and drink coffee*]
　　We need to get this boat fixed.
Al: Please, Andy, let me finish my coffee. I feel terrible.
　　　　　　　　　　　　　　　　　[*Cap lies back*]
Cap: I just want to lie here for now. You always make things so damn rosy. Can't we start tomorrow?
Andy: Let's start now. C'mon, Cap!
Cap: I can't believe you.
Andy: You've always been this way. Putting things off until they never get done; can't you see that! When you were a kid, you were the last one to lend a hand; even then you'd complain about one thing or another.
Cap: All right, all right, I've heard enough. I'll get my tools.
　　　　　　　　　　　　　　　　　[*He goes below*]
Al: Don't you think you were a little tough on him?
Andy: Believe me, that's the only language he understands. He'd just lie around until someone else did his work.

Cap *comes up the companionway with his tools and begins to adjust the halyards.* Al *tries to break the tension between the two.*

Al: How often do you have to varnish?

Cap: Every six months, the salt water and sun really take their toll.

It took me two months to varnish the main; it's eighty feet high. I had to hoist myself up and down in this little seat. What a pain in the ass!

[*He tests the tension of the halyards*]

I'll call this good. It isn't perfect, but it's a lot better than before.

Cap *climbs on the dock, which is cluttered with tools, and examines a rusted outboard engine.*

Cap: This outboard needs help.
Andy: Al's got the magic fingers.
Al: Why me?
Cap: It worked two years ago, but it got swamped in a storm.

[*They climb on the dock and Al disassembles the engine*]

I took it apart once, cleaned and lubed everything.
Al: Not everything!

Al *cleans off the heavy corrosion inside the carburetor. He pulls the starter. Nothing.*

Al: Something's frozen, give me the WD-40.

[*Cap passes the lubricant*]

Cap: It will be a miracle if it starts.

Al *sprays the carburetor, then pulls; pull, backfire, pull, backfire, ignition. The engine runs.*

Al (beaming): Let's try it out!

They climb into the zodiac and Andy *lowers the engine, but the dinghy begins to deflate and buckles in the center, causing the bow to raise straight up. Al scrambles onto the dock as* Cap *passes the outboard to* Andy.

Cap: I forgot about the leaky valves. Who knows what will be next!

Suddenly, a loud, moaning creak can be heard from the bowels of the yacht.

Cap: What the hell was that?
Al: It doesn't sound good to me!

Cap *climbs on the yacht and listens. Another moan echoes from below; then the floorboards creak and rise up around the mast step.*

Cap: Someone get me a flashlight, quick.

Al *pulls a flashlight out of his backpocket and shines it in his face.* Cap *grabs the light away and looks beneath the broken deck.*

Cap: Oh, my God, what's happening? Help me pull these floorboards up.
[*They begin to remove the floorboards*]
Cap (horrified): Look at that dry rot!
Al: Unbelievable!
Cap: Didn't I tell you it was one thing after another. I'm going to have to refit this piece of shit. Why me?
Al: We'll have to dig out the dry rot and reinforce it with fiberglass. Then we'll need to get some heavy gauge steel and bolt it to the floor. That should hold the mast.
Cap: I need a drink!
Al: You got a tape measure, Cap?

Cap *fumbles through a box full of nuts and bolts and finds a tape measure; the recoil is broken and the length of the tape is crammed into the box.*

Al: Nice tool.
[*Cap smiles faintly*]

Andy: C'mon Cap, cheer up! Nobody said this was going to be easy. You'll just have to get tough.
Al: Once the mast is securely in place, it'll probably be stronger than it was before.
Cap: I still don't understand. Why is this happening to me?

Scene iii. *Main Salon, two weeks later. . . .*

Andy *is finishing giving* Cap *a haircut*

Andy: You look like a new man.
Cap: I feel great too!

Cap *examines his hair in the mirror. He takes out an electric razor and shaves.*

Cap: We need to do some celebrating; this yacht is about ship-shape.

Cap *opens a bottle of rum, takes a healthy drink, and passes it to* Al. Al *takes a gulp.*

Al: Good stuff.
    [*They pass the bottle back and forth*]
Cap: What do you say we go to the CASINO tonight! I have three captains' uniforms. Hats, shirts, pants, the whole bit! Let's get dressed up and celebrate!
Al: Not me! Not a chance.
Cap: C'mon, Al, it will be fun. I'll get the uniforms.

Andy *puts his hand on* Al's *shoulder as* Cap *pulls clothes out of the closet.*

Andy: Listen, Buddy, women love a man in uniform.
    [*Al tries on the hat and admires himself in the mirror*]
Cap: You look like an admiral.
Al: You can't be serious.

Andy: I like these insignia things on the shoulders.
Cap: You'll be a hit, Andy!

[*Al squeezes into his shirt*]

Al: What do you think?
Cap: PERFECT!

Scene iv. *The inlet*

Our trio, dressed as captains, bounce in the zodiac as Cap *zig-zags through the inlet. As they approach the dock,* Cap *rams the zodiac into the bulkhead, practically throwing* Al *overboard; then on hands and knees, they crawl into the adjoining zodiacs and onto the docks.*

Scene v. *Casino*

Looking very official, Al, Andy *and* Cap *huddle together before making their grand entrance into the gambling hall.*

Al: This is crazy!
Cap: We can do it. Besides, who cares? We're just having fun; you look great! If I were alone, dressed like this, that would be one thing, but nobody will question the three of us!
Al: I'm going last. I'll hide behind you!

[*Cap starts in*]

The casino is crowded and noisy with lights flashing everywhere. The three captains walk between the tables, getting weird looks from the crowd. They find a table and seat themselves.

Karen, *a beautiful black waitress dressed in a white shirt, black tie, and black nylons, approaches.*

Karen: Hello, Cap. Where were you the other night?

[*Cap smiles coyly*]

Cap: Sorry, my brother just arrived.

[*Karen's cat eyes glimmer*]
Karen: Why the uniforms?
[*Cap winks*]
I can't believe you. You yachties are too much. Sherry and I waited a long time for you, my sailor friend. I'm afraid we're not happy with you.
[*Karen smiles at Al*]
Cap: What about tonight, after work?
[*Karen laughs*]
Karen: Sure.
Cap: Really?
[*Karen shakes her head in disbelief*]
Karen (to Al): You're cute.
[*She winks at him, then leaves*]
Al: Unbelievable!
Cap: Andy, let me borrow a couple of dollars. I feel lucky!
Andy: I thought you quit gambling.
Cap: I did, but just this once. I can't help myself.
Andy: Why do you have to gamble? I want to give you a chance; let's just enjoy ourselves tonight.
[*Knuckles, a security guard, short and fat, approaches Cap*]
Knuckles: Please come with me.
Cap (annoyed): You crazy?
[*Cap notices his name tag*]
Cap: Knuckles, what kind of name is that! Who are you?
Knuckles: You follow me.
Cap: This better be good.
[*Knuckles leads them through the crowd*]
Al: What's going on?
Andy: What's the problem?
Cap (disgusted): Who knows?
[*They enter a door marked "Casino Security"*]

Red Diamond, *a shady, suspicious character, sits behind a desk and* Rondo, *his seedy henchman, stands behind him.* Knuckles *blocks the door and pulls out his revolver.*

Cap (nervous): Wait one minute! What do you want?

Red: Don't you remember me? You sold me down the river on that condo project.
Cap: It wasn't my fault! You got the wrong guy!
[*Cap cowardly looks at Andy*]
Red (grinning): I can make your life very difficult, if you don't cooperate.
Cap (shocked): This really sucks!

Red *smiles, revealing a diamond, embedded in his front tooth. He pounds the desk.*

Red (shouting): Shut up! I want my money; otherwise I'll turn you over to my pals.
Cap (downtrodden): I can't believe this!
[*Cap looks at Andy*]
Cap: This isn't fair! I don't have that kind of money!
Red (sly): Captain has an expensive yacht. You can raise the money.
[*Cap's body goes limp. He puts his head in his hands*]
Cap: I need to use your phone.
Red (grins): Certainly, Captain.
[*Red pushes the phone toward him, Cap dials. Phone rings*]
Cap: PEACHES! This is Cap!
Peaches: Where are you, you jerk! I have half a mind to hang up.
Cap: Honey, please! I'm in trouble.
Peaches: Really. What's new?
Cap: I need twenty thousand dollars. FAST!
Peaches (laughing): I'm not helping you this time. Find somebody else.
Cap (softly): Please, honey.
Peaches: I haven't heard from you in six months!
Cap: Please, baby. I love you so much. I dream about you every night.
[*Al nudges Andy*]
Peaches (angry): All right, but this is the last time. Where are you?
Cap: Lakaya Casino, Freeport, BAHAMAS. I'm being framed!

[*She hangs up*]
Red: Shut up and make yourself comfortable, Captain. I'll be waiting for your girlfriend.
[*Red, Knuckles, and Rondo file out of the room*]
Andy (confused): What's going on?
[*Andy looks suspiciously at Cap*]
Cap: I hate this. This is how my whole life has been.
[*Cap pounds the desk*]
Cap: No! I can't believe this! I don't want to lose everything.
Al: What about us?
Andy: You've always had the way to make easy money. He'll kill you. You're nothing to him. Don't be a fool; he'll kill you. Give him his money back.

Scene vi. *Garden Café*

Unshaven and tired, Cap, Andy, *and* Al *drink coffee in their dirty, wrinkled uniforms.* Peaches, *an attractive, shapely young woman, acts distant as* Cap *tries to talk to her.*

Cap: Baby, I love you so much. Thanks for coming.
Peaches: So, how are you going to pay me back the twenty thousand dollars!
Cap: I'm being framed!
Andy: You've got to get a hold of yourself, Cap; there's a reason for what's happening to you. You might not want to admit it, but you brought this on yourself.
Cap: I'm tired of living hand to mouth. I want my share!
Peaches: The bank's looking for you, there's been investigators at my house, they want their yacht. What you're doing is wrong; you can't keep running!
Cap: No.
Andy: Give it up.
Cap: I've always been a loser; finally when I got into the real estate business, I go bust. How do you expect me to feel?
[*Cap laughs*]
Peaches: The guys at the race track were asking a lot of

questions at the club about you. They want their money too!

Cap: Man, this gives me a headache. How will I be able to pay all of them off?

Andy: You never told about this!

Peaches: You know you can't keep running. Try to understand, you must deal with this.

Cap: I'll figure something out!

Peaches: Oh, right. Right, Cap. I can see you've really listened to what I've said. I'm here to help you. What if they come after you?

Cap: I don't think they will.

Peaches: That's what you always say and that's half your problem. I'm starting to wonder why I'm here!

Cap: Easy, honey. It's been pretty rough around here without a woman! I wish things were normal. I feel like I'm spinning out of control.

I'm sorry I got everybody into this mess.

[*Cap paces back and forth*]

(*angry*) Those casino people were nothing more than a bunch of crooks.

Andy (serious): Forget about them! Let's return the yacht to the bank.

Red, Rondo, *and* Knuckles *inconspicuously slither into the café and enter the office.*

Cap (excited): Hey! Did you see that! Those were the thugs from the casino!

Al (wide-eyed): I can't believe it!

Andy: Let's get out of here!

Gunshots come from the office, and the four scramble to the floor and hide behind their table. Red *bursts through the office door, followed by* Knuckles. Rondo *trips as he comes through the doorway, and the suitcase he is carrying bounces toward* Cap.

A volley of gunfire erupts. Red, helplessly pinned down by gunfire, watches as Cap *retrieves the suitcase.*

Gunfire becomes heavy.

Cap *stuffs the contents of the suitcase into his pockets, then crawls between the tables and chairs, escapes. The others follow.*

Act II

Scene i. *Cap's Yacht*

Cap *is at the helm, as* Andy *releases the lines from the dock.* Al *and* Peaches *raise the main, and slowly the yacht moves out of the inlet and into the open ocean. As they sail away from the island,* Cap *takes the stolen money from beneath his shirt and hands it to* Peaches.

Cap: There's over one hundred thousand dollars! (*pause*) Looks like you get your money back, honey.
Al: This is incredible!
Cap (happy): Well, like I've always said, I was born to be rich!
Andy: You stole that money out of the suitcase!
Cap: We'll be far away by the time those thugs realize what happened! Call it what you will, I call it damn good luck!
Andy: Just keep your eyes open. We don't need any mishaps.

Al *goes below and reappears with a bottle of rum and four glasses. He pours a round.*

Al: A toast to Peaches, who set us free, and here we are upon the sea!
Andy: A toast to Peaches.
           [*They all raise their glasses and drink*]
Al: Where are we headed from here, Cap?
Cap: Jamaica, St. Maartin, South America.
           [*Cap raises his glass*]
Andy: I thought we were going to return the yacht to the bank!
Cap: I'll pay them off! (*pause*) To a life of adventure. All in favor!
Al (excitedly): Aye, aye!
Peaches (serious): Sounds like the same old story. You don't know where you're going!
Cap: I want everyone to know I have made a sound decision.
Peaches (groaning): Oh, no! Please spare me.

Cap: There will be difficult times on the ocean, we must all be fearless, together we will overcome!

Al: South it is! One for all and all for one.

[*Al and Cap clink glasses*]

Peaches: I've heard enough of this. I'm going forward for some fresh air. I'm about ready to get sick.

[*She goes forward*]

Cap: See! What did I tell you? Some temper, huh?

Andy: I don't think you know a good thing when you have it.

Cap: Sounds to me like you like her. Go ahead, be my guest. She's all yours.

Andy (annoyed): You pass her off like she's nothing! Why are you so afraid of loving someone?

Cap: I'm not! She just isn't right for me!

Andy: That's what you say about all of them.

Cap: No, I don't!

Andy: Listen to you. You're so damn stubborn.

Cap: I could never love her. Why don't you go up with her?

Andy: I'll go talk to her.

Cap: Tell her I'll fix dinner.

[*Andy goes forward*]

    South it is!

Al: Aye, aye, sir!

[*They toast*]

Peaches *sits on deck looking at the ocean as* Andy *approaches.*

Peaches: I heard what Cap said. It's okay. With guys like him, everything starts out great. Then, after a while, it gets weird. I don't know if I really know what love is about.

    I keep hoping that someday I'll find somebody. I know I must sound corny, but . . .

Andy: Cap's a good guy, he's afraid to open his heart. He's sort of a lost soul, but you're not! I can feel that from you.

Peaches: Thanks.

[*He takes her hand in his*]

Andy: There's something special about you.

Scene ii. *At sea*

Unbeknownst to Cap *and his crew, a pirate ship appears on the horizon.* Rondo *is at the helm.* Red *searches in the ice chest for food.*

Red: This is a disgusting mess.
  [*Knuckles has a sudden involuntary facial contraction*]
Knuckles: So what!
Red: Look at this bread! You spastic!
Red *throws the loaf of moldy bread and hits* Knuckles *squarely in the head.*
Red: Maybe that will make your brain grow! (*pause*) How did I end up with two idiots?
  [*He raises his pistol and points it at them*]
Red: Maybe I should shoot both of you!
Rondo: Shoot Knuckles.
Red: Just fix me something to eat. I'm starving.
Knuckles: When are we going to catch them, Boss?
Red: What do you think I'm working on?
  [*Rondo picks up a butcher knife*]
Rondo: I'll slice that fat guy in half!
Red: If everything goes as planned, we'll have them by tomorrow night!

Scene iii. *Cap's yacht effortlessly sails through the blue sea*

Cap: This is the way man is meant to live!
  [*Andy shades his eyes from the brilliant sun*]
Andy: Quick, where are the binoculars?
Al: Anything wrong?
  [*Al passes the binoculars*]
Andy: Look alive, Cap!
  [*Andy makes an adjustment*]
Andy (alarmed): A reef!
Cap: A what? Give me those!

Suddenly the yacht lurches. The boom swings wild, and everyone falls down. Screams from below. Peaches comes on deck.

Cap (horrified): What's happened?
Andy: We've gone aground!
Peaches: I knew you should never have taken that money!
Cap (head in hands): Oh, shit! Why me?
      [*The boom continues to swing wildly*]
Al (frantic): Oh, God! What should we do?
     [*Cap hangs over the rail to look for damage*]
Andy: I'm going to see if we're taking on water!
        [*Andy goes below deck*]
Peaches (disgusted): I thought you knew where you were going, Captain!
     [*Cap ignores her as Al peeks over the side*]
Al: We're in four feet of water! What should we do?
        [*Andy comes on deck*]
Andy: The hull seems to be okay. There's no water. I think we should set an anchor and winch her off!
Al (horrified): I don't want to die.
Cap: Get up, fatso! You're sitting on the anchor.
Peaches (disgusted): I can't believe you!
Cap (screaming at Al): You're on the anchor, shithead. Where are your goddamn ears?
   [*Peaches helps Al to the opposite side of the cockpit*]
Andy: Calm down, Cap!

Andy *takes an anchor out from below the seat and lowers it into the zodiac. As* Cap *paces the deck,* Andy *motors away from the yacht to set the anchor.*

Al: What am I doing out here?
Peaches: Just relax, Al!
Al: How could this happen to us? I wasn't cut out for this!
Peaches: Think positive.

Andy *drops the anchor off the zodiac, and* Cap *begins to winch in the line.*

Al: Is it working?
Cap: We need a big tide to lift us off this shoal. Problem is there's no tide.
Al: Impossible! There's tide everywhere!
Cap: Well, not here, Buddy!
Al: C'mon, there must be a little change.
Cap: There's not, bonehead! Just leave me alone.
[*Peaches pulls Al to the side*]
Al: Man, I'm starting to wonder about this guy. How did he ever get a captain's license?
Peaches: Just leave him alone. He's got a lot on his mind.
Al: Do you think we're going to drown? I think I can see sharks circling the boat.
Cap: Oh, stop your moaning! This is the best thing that ever happened to you; maybe you'll lose a few pounds! You get out of your element and you fall apart. Tighten up!
Al (worried): I'm too young to die!
Cap (laughing): Die? You will die if you don't shut up!

As Andy *comes on deck,* Cap *goes after* Al *with the winch handle.*

Cap: You big pussy!
[*Andy separates the two*]
Al: You're a pussy, Cap!
Andy: You're not going to die, Al! I'll get us out of here!
[*Andy takes the handle from Cap and winches*]
Cap (to himself): Where's Peaches? Peaches! Peaches! Now where did she go?
[*Peaches appears*]
Cap: We're really stuck.
Peaches: This isn't the first time. Cap's had this happen a couple of times before, huh, Cap?
Cap (disgusted): I don't want to talk about it!
[*He scratches his head*]

Cap (excited): Wait a minute. Look, I think we're moving!
Peaches: You're kidding!
Cap (wide-eyed): No, really!
Al: It's a miracle.

[*The sails begin to fill*]

Peaches: I can't believe it!
Cap (shouting): Damn!

[*Slowly the yacht pulls off the shoal and sails away*]

Al: We're going to be O.K.!

[*Al hugs Cap*]

Cap (shouting): You did it, Andy! You got us off!

[*Cap takes the helm*]

Cap: Al, pay attention! This is your chance to become a real sailor. Go to the bow and use your hands and point where the shallow water is.
Al: Aye, aye, sir.

Al *salutes, then cautiously works his way to the bow and helps direct* Cap *out of the shallow waters.*

Scene iv. *Pirate ship*

Red *searches the horizon with a spyglass.*

Red (excitedly): I see them! Get ready to come about!

Knuckles *turns the wheel hard as* Rondo *fumbles with the lines and the jib and foresails tangle in the rigging. The boom swings overhead, narrowly missing* Red.

Red (outraged): Idiot! You'll pay for this, Rondo.
Knuckles (smirking): Let me have the honor, Boss!

[*Red swings the spyglass at Rondo*]

Red (shouting): Get up there and free those sails!

Rondo *works his way forward and cuts the lines. As the pirate ship loses speed,* Cap's *yacht fades into the distance.*

Scene v. *The doldrums*

Time stand's still beneath the relentless sun. The ocean is flat, no wind. Cap *stands on the bow staring ahead.* Al, *sweating heavily, tries to hide from the sun beneath a sail cover.*

Peaches: I can't believe Cap. He's crazy to think he's going to get away with this!
Andy: Who knows what's going on inside that head of his!
Peaches: He says he wants to change. I don't know. I've got a funny feeling.

Al, *drenched with perspiration, sticks his head out from beneath the sail cover.*

Al: Dear God, please save me from this heat. I'm boiling!
Andy: Go take a shower, you'll feel better!
                        [*Al staggers to his feet*]
Peaches: Hang in there, Al.
Al: Yeah, after I'm dead!
                              [*Al goes below*]
Peaches: How long will this weather last?
Andy: It should break, but don't you love how unpredictable things are on the ocean.
Peaches: You sound like your brother!

Suddenly, a blast of wind fills the sails and the yacht heels over, throwing Andy *on top of* Peaches.

Al (screaming from below): Hellllp!

Slowly the yacht comes upright, and Cap *hurriedly returns to the helm.*

Cap (excitedly): Thar' she blows! Damn, we got a big one coming. Al, get up here quick!
                  [*Al staggers on deck; he looks frantic*]
   I think we better reef all the sails!

Peaches (disgusted): We've been in these doldrums over forty-eight hours! Now, you're saying we should reef the sails! Are you nuts?

Cap (serious): I sense it; look at those black clouds moving our way!

[*They all look*]

Al (nervous): I've never seen a sky like that!

Andy: It does look sort of strange.

Cap: Peaches, go below and batten everything down; then bring up the life jackets and rain gear. I'm not going into this thing unprepared!

[*Peaches goes below*]

Al (nervous): Maybe we should call the Coast Guard!

[*Cap laughs*]

Andy: I'll see if I can get any weather information on the radio.

Cap (serious): Go ahead, but I doubt you'll get anything. Besides, we're in it now. She's coming. I can feel it. She'll be a doozy all right!

[*It begins to rain as Andy goes below*]

Al (prayerful): Please, God, don't let me die.

Cap (smiling): Go tell your mother; don't get yellow now. This is Mother Sea! It makes me feel alive. C'mon, baby, rock me!

A wave breaks over the bow. Al, horrified, clings to the safety line.

Al (afraid): Please, take me to shore!

Cap (shouting): Peaches, hurry up!

Peaches *comes on deck and passes out rain jackets.* Andy *follows, carrying the life vests.*

Andy: Major tropical depression moving this way. The radio says we'll be feeling the effects in five hours; she'll be blowing full force by tonight.

[*The sky blackens*]

Al: This is all your fault, Cap!

Cap: Talk like that and I'll throw you overboard, Fatty. *(pause)* I'm going forward to take down the sails. Andy, you take the helm, steer her into the wind.

[*Cap carefully moves forward*]

Al: I feel sick. *Imagine, a hurricane!*
Andy: Maybe you should go below and get some rest while you can.
Al: Do you really think a storm is coming? Maybe it'll miss us!
Andy: Let's hope that mast HOLDS!

The wind becomes vicious, causing the yacht to heel at an extreme angle.

Al (screaming): Ahhh . . .

Cap *returns to the cockpit, takes the wheel, and gives it a hard turn.*

Peaches (shouting): Now what?
Cap: Who knows?

The yacht comes about and a huge wave breaks over the boat. Peaches *loses her balance and goes overboard.*

Peaches (screaming): Help! Help me! Help me!
Cap: She's gone! Can you see her?

Peaches's *head bobs between the waves. Helplessly, she floats away from the yacht.*

Al: Oh, my God!
Andy (shouting/pointing): There she is.

Andy *takes off his life jacket and slicker and strips to his shorts.*

Cap: Be careful! It's pretty wild out there!

Andy *goes over the rail into the ocean. Foamy blue green waves break over* Peaches *as she struggles to remain on the surface.* Andy *swims hard, but has difficulty in the heavy swell. He swims over a wave and out of sight.*

Cap *steers the yacht directly into the wind and slows the boat enough for* Al *to throw them a lifesling. A wave hurls them together and* Peaches *clings tightly to* Andy *as he recovers the floatation collar. They grasp it for dear life as* Al *pulls them alongside.*

Scene vi. *Pirate ship*

The full fury of the storm has hit. Red *steers through the chopping sea.*

Rondo *(shouting):* We're taking a ton of water; the bilge pump can't handle it!
Red *(shouting):* Get back down there and hand-pump, shithead! We've almost got them!

Suddenly, the mast snaps and the sail crashes into the sea. The ship lists, and the bow goes skyward. Red *pounds his fist over* Knuckles's *head.*

Red: Look what you've done!

As the pirate ship begins to sink, they scramble over the rail and into the rowboat. Red *watches helplessly as his ship disappears beneath the sea.*

Red: Pull on those bloody oars, you meatheads. Cap's getting away!
Rondo: I can't go any further.
Knuckles: Water, water, or I'll die!
 [*Red draws his pistol*]
Red *(smirking):* Be quick at those oars or I'll feed you to the sharks!

Act III

Scene i. *As the sun breaks through the cloudy sky, we find* Cap's *yacht at anchor off an island*

The zodiac has been taken ashore and is pulled up on the beach. Our four exhausted sailors lie on the sand still shaken from their ordeal.

Al: I don't care if it's only a sandbar. Thank God, I'm saved! I'm so glad to get off that damn boat!
Cap: Oh, c'mon, buddy. Don't tell me you didn't enjoy it.
Al: I could have lived without it! I've had enough!
Andy: I have to admit, Cap, you got us through the worst.
    [*Cap searches the island through his binoculars*]
Al: I can't believe how good it feels to have my feet on solid ground. My body feels like it's still rocking.
Cap: I can imagine with a body like yours!
Al: I don't care what you say. Thank goodness I'll never have to go to sea again!
Peaches: Look! Someone's coming!
Al: SAVED!
    [*Al jumps to his feet and waves his arms madly*]

Violet, *a black woman carrying a basket of fruit and a stalk of bananas on her head, approaches.*

Violet: Yes suh! May I help you?
Al: Food! Bananas!

She puts down her goods and gives Al *a banana, which he devours.*

Violet: You try one of *these* sweet babies, just like candy, just like candy.
    [*She peels him an orange*]
Al: I'll take ten pounds.

Violet: Oh, yes, these keep you strong.
> [*She smiles at Al as she weighs the oranges*]

Here, you must try the avocado. Very good, ripe and tender the way you like it. Now you take maybe this many!
> [*She fills a bag with avocados*]

Al: Okay, good, yes, thanks!
Peaches: We need provisions for four people.
Violet: Yeah, I can handle it, Miss. Smell my melons. I make you a good deal.
> [*She passes them around*]

Did you all just sail in?
Al: Yes, madam. We just arrived from the Bahamas. Please! I would rather not talk about it. Perhaps you have an extra room. I don't need anything fancy, just something, anything.
> [*She laughs*]

Violet (compassionate): You poor man. Perhaps I can help you.
Al (excited): Something with running water?
Violet: My brother has a place, but it needs a lot of work. If you like, I'll take you to meet him.
Al: You are very kind!
Peaches: Are you sure about this! What about the yacht?

Cap *looks out in the bay. His yacht floats peacefully at anchor.*

Cap: Looks okay to me.
Andy: It'll be fine. Don't worry.
Violet (dreamy to Al): You have gentle eyes.
> [*She pinches his cheek*]

Violet: Come, I'll show you.
> [*They follow her down the beach*]

Como, *a black Rastafarian, colorfully dressed, sits on porch of his grass-roofed shack;* Violet *approaches with her befriended sailors.*

Como: Hello, darling.
> [*He stands and greets her*]

Who be these white Brothers and Sister?

Al: SAILORS looking for a port in a storm.

Violet: They need a place to stay, Brother.

Como: Certainly, my friends. I would like to help you! C'mon, I'll show you.

They follow Como *down a trail, which descends toward the ocean and continues through a jungle of beautiful flowers; beyond is a bungalow surrounded by coconut trees with the blue ocean in the background.*

Cap: Paradise!

Peaches: This is beautiful!
  [*Peaches has a dreamy look as she moves close to Andy*]
  I guess all the madness has been worth it. I'm glad to be here.
            [*Al nervously takes Cap aside*]

Al: We're the only white guys I've seen. Do you think we'll be okay?

Cap: C'mon, what do you think is going to happen?

Violet (to Peaches): Don't worry, honey. I'll help you clean up!

Peaches: I love it!

Al: We'll take it!
            [*Al hugs Como*]

Peaches: I can't believe it's real.
            [*She kisses Andy*]

Cap: I was getting tired of the sailor life. It's good to be on dry land! No phone calls, no condos, no bills.

Al: You got that right!

Violet *picks a mango off the tree, peels it, and hands it to* Al.

Violet: Here, try this, darling.
                    [*Al eats*]

Al: I've never tasted anything like this. I could stay here forever!

Violet: Hallelujah.
            [*She hugs Al*]

Scene ii. *A sleazy bar*

A den of thieves, dark and dingy. A Stripper *moves sensuously to the music.* Red *speaks with the* Bartender.

Bartender: What will it be, mister?
Red: I'm looking for Mole.

Bartender *motions toward* Mole, *a fat man with no neck, sitting alone in the corner.* Red *and his men approach the* Mole.

Red: Long time no see. You remember my boys?
Mole: How could I forget them?
                         [*Rondo and Knuckles smirk*]
   I'll get you something to drink.
                         [*He shouts to Waitress*]
   Bring my friends rum. What can I do for you, Red?
Red: I need to find somebody. I think he's on the island.
   [*The Waitress returns with a bottle of rum and glasses*]
                         [*Mole pours a round*]
   I want this guy found immediately!
                         [*He pounds the table*]
Mole: Listen, Red, you might as well relax. We'll look tomorrow.
                         [*The Stripper approaches the table*]
   Enjoy the scenery.
                   [*Rondo and Knuckles smirk at each other*]
Knuckles: Wow!

Scene iii. *Beach bungalow*

As the sun sets, Andy *and* Peaches *lie in a hammock, looking out at the ocean.*

Andy: I couldn't sleep last night. I kept thinking about you.
Peaches: Don't tell me that unless you mean it.
Andy: Well, it's true. I want to try and make it work between
   you and me.

Peaches: I've heard this all before.
> [*Peaches shakes her head*]

Andy: C'mon, let's try!

Peaches: Have you told your brother how you feel about me?

Andy: He's getting the idea. I'm serious. Please believe me.

Peaches: Just give me some time. I need to think it out. C'mon lover boy, I'll make you some Creole food. It'll be good for your soul.

Later that same night, Al *and* Cap *wait to be seated at a dinner club in town.*

Hostess: Just the two of you this evening?

Cap (smiling): Unless *you* would like to join us.
> [*Hostess leads them to the table*]

Hostess: Would you care to order drinks?

Cap: Thank you, sweets. A bottle of your best Beaujolais.
> [*She leaves*]

Al: You're crazy bringing us in here! How in the hell are we going to pay for it?
> [*Cap brings out a wad of hundred-dollar bills*]

Cap: You worry too much.
> [*Al puts his head in his hands*]

Cap: Relax. Remember, we're celebrating!

Al *and* Cap *sip their wine as the* Waitress *serves them the first course.*

Cap: I'm beginning to feel antsy stuck in one spot, I'm ready to ship out. You wanna come?

Al: No thanks, Captain. I'm happy where I am. The sailor's life is not for me. I like lying around in the sand and cooling off in the ocean.

Cap: Ah, you landlubbers are all alike—afraid of a little adventure. There's no action around here; everybody moves too *slow*. The natives on this island act like there's no tomorrow.

Al: You got to learn how to relax.

[*Cap pours himself a glass of wine and downs it*]
Your mind jumps around from one thing to another, you got a busy brain, slow down!

Cap: What are you talking about? (*pause*) Listen, I got this great idea how to make a ton of money, easy money! All I got to do is get back to the mainland. This is a sure shot, guaranteed one hundred percent return!

[*Al starts to eat his salad*]
You're just afraid to take a little chance. You're just like my brother. Life's going to slip you by, Big Boy.

Al (mad): You better just watch out! Last hair-brained idea you had you lost everything.

Cap: That was the last time, this idea is a cinch, I can't miss.

After a five-course meal Cap *pays the bill with a couple of hundred-dollar bills.*

Al: I feel drunk.

Cap: You are drunk and so am I. We're two drunk skunks on the lam.

Al: There's one problem. How are we going to find our way back?

Cap: I have good directional sensory.

[*Cap sniffs the air*]

Al: Okay, Captain, you lead and I'll follow.

As they leave the dinner club and start down the street they pass Rondo *and* Knuckles, *who are having a violent fist fight. In between punches . . .*

Rondo: Those guys look familiar to you?

Knuckles: How should I know, I've never been here before.

Rondo: Better follow 'em.

Act IV

Scene i. Red's *goons have led him to where they followed* Cap *and* Al *the night before.*

Knuckles: There's the captain's hideout dead ahead.
Rondo: Dead ahead. I like that!
[*Rondo laughs*]
Red: Shut up, you fool!
[*They approach the bungalow, but no one is in sight*]
Search the place, that money's got to be here somewhere.

Red *viciously kicks in the door and begins tearing things apart as he desperately searches for his money.*

Knuckles: I can't find anything.
Rondo: Likewise, Boss.
Red: It's got to be here someplace; besides, he'll show up sooner or later.
Knuckles: Then we'll take care of him once and for all, huh, Boss?
Red: I don't know what I would do without you. (*pause*) Now, let's turn the place upside down!

In no time the bungalow is in total shambles. Outside Al, Cap, Peaches *and* Violet *merrily stroll down the beach toward the bungalow.* Red *and his men wait until the last minute then burst out from behind the door.* Red *points his pistol at* Cap.

Red (calm): Okay, Captain, where's my money?
Cap: You crook!
[*Red slaps Cap around*]
Al: Pick on somebody your own size!
[*Rondo punches Al in the stomach*]
Al (nervous): Just give him the money back, Cap!
Red: Listen to your fat friend, Captain!

Cap (disgusted): I don't have it with me. I've hidden it!

[*Red slaps Cap around*]

Peaches: Stop! I know where the money is!

Cap: Don't tell him!

Red (sly): So, my pretty one.

Peaches: I'll need some time, but if you promise to leave Cap alone, I'll get you the money!

Red: You've got my word! I'll let you go, but if you cross me, I'll slit their throats.

[*Knuckles and Rondo smirk*]

I'll give you till sunup. We'll be at the old sugar plantation. Remember, no foul-ups, or . . .

[*Red runs his fingers under his throat*]

Scene ii. *Reggae Club*

Andy *listens to* Como's Reggae band. Peaches *enters and sinks down beside him.*

Andy: What's happened? Where are the others?

Alarmed, Andy *grabs* Peaches *by the shoulders and shakes her. The music stops.*

Andy: What's going on?

Peaches: Red Diamond has them. He wants his money. He told me no screw-ups or he'd slit their throats! (*pause*) He's never going to leave us alone.

[*Como approaches*]

Como: What's happened? Where's my sister?

[*Club quiets*]

Peaches: Red Diamond has them!

Como (confused): What's this all about?

Peaches: Diamond's holding them hostage at the sugar plantation; he told me no screw-ups or he'd slit their necks.

Como (yelling): C'mon brothers. Violet's in trouble!

[*Club empties*]

Scene iii. *Sugar Plantation*

As the sun burns off the morning dew, the remains of a dilapidated sugar refinery appear. Rotten wood beams sag beneath the rusted roof. In the basement Violet, Al, *and* Cap *are tied, spread-eagled against a wall as* Knuckles *stands guard.* Red Diamond *and* Rondo *lurk on a platform above our heros.* Knuckles *pushes his pistol against* Al's *stomach.*

Knuckles: C'mon, fat boy. Tell me where the money is, otherwise, I spill your guts all over the place.
Violet: Leave him alone, you. Can't you see he doesn't know anything!
Knuckles: Okay my little pussy, maybe you'll tell me.
[*Knuckles slaps Al*]
Cap: Stop! You'll get your money.

Knuckles *laughs as he scratches the side of his face with the barrel of his pistol.*

Knuckles (smirking): That's not all I'll get; your little Peaches is a tasty morsel.

Unbeknownst to the three villains, Como *and the* Black Brothers *are on the roof beams securing ropes around their waists. They lower themselves towards* Red *and* Rondo. Rondo *is caught totally off guard and becomes entangled in ropes, but* Red *escapes into the jungle. A volley of gunfire erupts.*

Al (alarmed): I don't want to die!
Knuckles: Die! You will die, Fat Boy!
Violet (prayerful): I walk in the valley. . . .

Andy *enters and surprises* Knuckles, *knocking him to the ground.*

Al (wide-eyed): It's a miracle. I can't believe it!
Cap (shouting): Damn!

Al: We're going to be okay, Violet!
Andy: Let's get out of here.
[*Suddenly Red appears holding a pistol*]
Red: Surprise!
[*Red cocks his gun*]
Don't anybody move! Now, where's my money?

Como *swings down out of nowhere, knocking the gun out of* Red*'s hand and* Andy *recovers the pistol.*

Violet: Praise the Lord!
Andy: Let's gather up these goons and deliver them to the local authorities.
Cap: I say let's finish them off right here and now!
Violet (to Al): Oh, Darling, my prayers have been answered.
[*She hugs Al*]
Red (to Cap): You're nothing but white trash.
Cap: As I've always said, crime doesn't pay!

Scene iv. *Cap's yacht*

Al, Cap, Peaches, Andy *and* Violet *sit beneath the bemni as the sailboat floats peacefully at anchor.*

Peaches: Well, at last those criminals are behind bars. Did you know Red Diamonds was on the FBI's list?
Al: Unbelievable.
Andy: Are you sorry you had to return the stolen money, Cap?
Cap: Naw! I took out the twenty thousand for Peaches, and I sent some to the bank. Now, I'm all caught up on the yacht payments. I'm sorry for what I've done in the past. I want to try and make my life work! There must be something wrong with me for treating everyone the way I did.
Al: I don't believe it.
Violet: Be nice, darling.
Andy: Peaches and I have an announcement. We plan to get married.

Violet: I'm so glad for you two children.

> [*She hugs Peaches*]

Cap: Congratulations! You are perfect for each other.

> [*Cap kisses Peaches on the cheek*]

Peaches: What about you, Cap? What are you going to do?

Cap: I'm going to fix my yacht; then, I'm not sure. Maybe I'll sail her to Rio.

Al: Don't ask me to come. I'm staying right here on this island. Como said if I practiced playing the steel drum, maybe I could play with his band.

Cap: This is a great day.

Andy: Oh, here's something that came in the mail for you.

> [*Cap opens the letter*]

Cap (horrified): It's from the I.R.S. They want TEN THOUSAND DOLLARS in back taxes!

He crumples the letter up and tosses it into the garbage can.

Cap: Who cares? They'll never find me!

> [*Cap turns on the radio*]

Radio Announcer: Thousands of spectators watch as jockeys ride thoroughbreds onto the track and line the horses up in the starting gate. The last horse enters the gate. The bell rings.

And they're off. Down the first stretch, it's Shilo at the front of the pack, followed by . . . Ramrod and Bingo, then Adam T. and Zoey. Following the field is Lonesome Boy! As the horses pass the quarter mile marker.

And it's Ramrod, then Bingo, with Shilo running third, followed by Zoey and Adam T., then Lonesome Boy.

Cap: C'mon, Ramrod! You got 'em, honey! C'mon home. Home to papa.

Radio Announcer: It's Ramrod by a head, then Adam T. and Zoey. It's Zoey and Adam T. challenging Ramrod!

Cap (yelling): Yes! Yes!

Radio Announcer: It's Ramrod, Zoey and Adam T. Results remain unofficial until the final posting.

> [*Cap anxiously waits*]

Radio Announcer: The results are final, it's Ramrod, Zoey, and Adam T.

Cap *pulls the winning ticket from his pocket and lovingly kisses it.*